Under the Magnolia Tree

Richard D. Ashe, Ph.D

authorHOUSE®

AuthorHouse™
1663 Liberty Drive
Bloomington, IN 47403
www.authorhouse.com
Phone: 1 (800) 839-8640

Published by AuthorHouse 03/02/2015

ISBN: 978-1-4969-7049-7 (sc)
ISBN: 978-1-4969-7048-0 (hc)
ISBN: 978-1-4969-7047-3 (e)

Library of Congress Control Number: 2015902592

Print information available on the last page.

TABLE OF CONTENTS

PREFACE

First and foremost, I wish to give thanks to my Lord and Savior for restoring my health and for giving me strength, courage and wisdom to complete the "Magnolia Book Project," **Under the Magnolia Tree.**

This writer is quite aware of the fact that when high school or college alumni usually get together at homecoming activities or other gatherings, inevitably, they share their "yesteryear memories." These reflective memories, no doubt can run the sphere of hilarious anecdote tales that have mind boggling conclusions.

Therefore, the intent of **Under the Magnolia Tree** seeks to provide a scholarly collection of information, humorous, inspirational and motivational memories of Stillman College alumni. Hopefully and prayerfully the book will inspire, and energize young readers to set and accomplish their goals regardless of what may appear to be insurmountable odds.

This book includes a synopsis of Stillman's historical legacy during the past fifty years. This is presented with facts and a collection of student photos.

Readers may also note that the author has included a couple of articles of non- Stillmanites. These articles were included because of their unique and motivational nature. A case in point is Pinkney Mosley's article, "A Pilot's Incredible Experiences." (Overcoming Great Odds) This article was included because the content of his message is not only extraordinary but powerful and enlightening.

The book also includes a passionate plea for HBCU graduates to rededicate their support for their alma mater in order to insure a delightful and lasting legacy.

If any part of **Under the Magnolia Tree** causes the reader to smile, laugh, motivate, or reflect on situations of past, present or future, then the author's objective will have been achieved.

FOREWORD

When my friend, neighbor and fellow Stillmanite, Richard Ashe informed me that he was undertaking the task of writing his fourth book which included a collection of personal, humorous, and motivational articles from Stillman College alumni, I made a commitment to participate in the book project. Needless to say, I had no idea that my role would be to write the Foreword for his book, **Under the Magnolia Tree**. In other words, my task is to introduce Dr. Richard D. Ashe to the world. For this honor, I am deeply grateful and appreciative.

Over the years I have had the opportunity to observe his educational maturity, professionalism, work ethics and his dedication to support his alma mater, HBCU schools and other institutions of higher learning. His rise from having just meager resources and humble background experiences to become the author of four books is not only awesome but inspiring.

Upon Dr. Ashe's retirement from the educational school system as a school administrator, he began to volunteer his services to community causes. He also began to write skits and short plays for the enjoyment and entertainment of senior citizens. Recently, a group of Stillman alumni and I attended a play that he wrote, directed and performed one of the play's central characters. Not only were we thoroughly entertained by the production and performance, we were also intrigued by Dr. Ashe's talent and acting skills. The title of the play is **"Judgment Day at Pearlie Gate Court."**

I am convinced that the readers of **Under the Magnolia Tree** will be mesmerized by the compilation of personal stories, spiritual sermons and poetry that the book renders. This book will also allow readers to compare their college and youthful experiences with the authors who submitted articles for the magnolia book project.

Therefore, I am pleased to request that this book become a must read for past and present college students, book clubs, casual readers, and senior citizens. You will be delighted to read, own and appreciate every aspect of this literary jewel, **Under the Magnolia Tree.**

Alice Blue Hamilton

Alice B. Hamilton is a 1967 graduate of Stillman College. She is also President of the Stillman College Atlanta Alumni Association.

DEDICATION

For decades, whenever I or my local alumni chapter members needed facts or clarifications related to Stillman activities, we could always rely on Annie Mary Gray for details. Her service to Stillman alumni, faculty and students are too numerous to mention. However, I will mention a few to highlight the depth of her involvement.

During her tenure at Stillman, she has served in positions as:

Secretary to Faculty
Secretary to the Division of Social Sciences
Secretary to the Dean of the College
Secretary to the Office of the President
Alumni Communications Assistant

Perhaps Ms. Gray's Stillman legacy is best represented by what her fellow co-workers say about her:

"Annie Mary Gray is beautiful, kind, loyal and compassionate. The love she shows to her family, friends and co-workers is a clear reflection of her character and sets a shining example for all who are blessed to be in her presence."

Mary Sood, Director of Marketing & PR

"Annie Mary Gray is a permanent fixture here at the College much like the Magnolias or our motto. When I was working as a recruiter, I would always share her story with potential recruits of how Ms. Gray was born at Stillman, graduated from Stillman, and continues to work here! They would be amazed and I would express how dedicated to the College she is, and how much she loves it. She always has a friendly smile for all who enter her office and is more energetic than most people who are half her age! Ms. Gray is always willing to lend a helping hand and I thoroughly enjoy working with her."

Cristi Hitt, Director of Scholarship Programs

"I am blessed to work with a loyal and dedicated co-worker, Ms. Annie Mary Gray. She has a pleasing personality and serves humanity by always helping others. We have worked together for over 35 years and I have learned to truly appreciate her words of wisdom and thoughtfulness. May God continue to bless Ms. Gray."

Luvenia Cain, Data Manager of Institutional Advancement

On behalf of the entire Stillmanite Nation, this author is proud to dedicate the first edition of **<u>Under The Magnolia Tree</u>** to Ms. Annie Mary Gray.

(Excerpts of a "Tuscaloosa News" article is presented in Chapter Four.)

MESSAGE FROM THE NATIONAL ALUMNI PRESIDENT

For years, alumni have been returning regularly and enthusiastically to Stillman to celebrate the many different reunions. A number of us make this sentimental journey; some travel great distances and others from just around the corner. But we come with a unified purpose: the love of Stillman College.

A big part of the celebration always involves sharing memories under the beautiful magnolia trees that adorn our beloved Stillman campus. Today, in our exchanges and encounters, we rediscover our younger selves in these memories, which bring us closer and reignites old friendships and alliances.

The stories we share, verbal or written are worth more than any news article or ranking of our school, as favorable as it may be.

Richard D. Ashe, Ph.D

Alumni support and achievement are our most treasured assets and celebrating <u>Under the Magnolia Tree</u> provides an occasion for us to reflect on the wonderful aesthetics of tradition.

As you turn these pages, I hope that it transports you back to those student days of creating memories under the canopy of trees where your dreams first took flight. And there is no doubt that for Dr. Ashe, writing this book was a labor of love for all alumni.

"Thank you for Sharing"

Jean A. Wilson-Sykes '90
NAASC Inc., President (2010-2015)

ACKNOWLEDGEMENTS

Several years ago, my friend and fellow Stillmanite, Max Parker encouraged me to write a book or play about memories of Stillman College. After numerous requests and his insistence, I finally took the challenge to undertake this awesome task. I'm glad I did because this literary journey has not only been exciting, but a distinct privilege and honor. This book would not have been possible without the contributions of the Stillman College alumni who shared their Stillman experiences as students.

For the development and production of **Under the Magnolia Tree,** I feel and owe a deep sense of gratitude to:

Robert Heath, Stillman College Archivist and Dean of Sheppard Library for his wisdom, assistance and numerous suggestions.

Annie Mary Gray for providing reliable data for this project and responding to numerous requests.

Anthony Holloman, who graciously provided leadership for securing technical and editing assistance necessary for the magnolia book project.

Luvenia Cain for providing research and assistance.

Luanne Baker for always providing appropriate material and contacts when needed and requested.

Esther Lawrence for her role as consultant to the magnolia book project.

Charlotte Mercadel for providing crucial information and serving as a major source of support for this project.

Tristen Simpson for providing one-of-a-kind photo and computer expertise.

Crystal Mealer and Evelyn King for assisting with the photo arrangements.

Laura Smith for providing her talented editing skills for the project.

John Carter of AuthorHouse for his assistance with the book submission process.

James Tate for being a loyal friend whose memory of childhood days is remarkable. His suggestions for the book project proved to be noteworthy.

Dr. Nathan Essex, an outstanding educator and great friend for sharing his wisdom on many issues over the years.

Felders Photography Studio for putting the final professional touch to the photo collages.

Elizabeth Baptist Church Hospitality members, Annie Wright, Sharmain Green, Valerie Roberts, and Sandra Fletcher for their support and prayers for the success of **Under the Magnolia Tree.**

Irene Richardson, Executive Director of Quality Living Services for Seniors, who invited me to become an active volunteer participant.

My late grandmother, Carrie Fowler who helped to teach me to be respectful to everyone and make choices that will keep me out of trouble.

The memory of my father, Clifton Ashe Sr. who taught his children to work and walk with dignity. His response to humorous information was "Well, I'm sorry now!"

My late mother, Marguerite Ashe-Brown who insisted that my siblings and I "do the best job that we can on an assigned task." She also encouraged her children to own up to the good or poor choices that we made by saying, "That's your little red wagon, so push or pull it." and " Be able to stand on your own indignity."

My wife Dorothy, who provided support, patience and suggestions.

My daughter Michelle, for providing computer and clerical assistance throughout the book process.

My sons, Charles and Chris, who are men of great character and have been a blessing to me.

My delightful grandchildren, Ciara, Jordan, Myles and Kaniya.

My Sister Jean, who keeps the family lifted up in prayer.

My brother Benny, whose Christian spirit and work ethic is one of a kind.

My brother, Leonard, who made the basketball "sky hook" fashionable long before Kareem Abdul Jabbar came on the sport scene. Appreciated is his love for me, his youngest brother.

My nieces, Maxine, Marilyn, Barbara, Sherry, Sylvia, Carol, Margaret, and Irene who are quick to give me tips on how to stay healthy; and for their greetings sent to me each year during special occasions.

My talented nephews, Ashley Jackson, Leory Shade, Jr. and Sean Brown who are quick to lend a helping hand to others who are in need.

My dear cousins, Annette Gipson and Charles Caldwell, who always lend support for my literary endeavors and family projects.

ABOUT THE AUTHOR

Dr. Richard Ashe is a native of Marion, North Carolina, where he received his elementary and secondary education. He received his Bachelor's degree from Stillman College, his Master's degree from Indiana University, and his Educational Specialist degree from 'The University of Alabama, where he was elected to Phi Delta Kappa Honorary Fraternity. He attained his Ph.D degree from The University of Minnesota.

He served as president or chairman of the board on several educational, community and social organizations. The Martin Luther King Jr. Center in St. Paul, Minnesota recognized his commitment to the community by awarding him a key for outstanding leadership and community service. The 100 Black Men of Atlanta, South Metro Chapter awarded him the NAACP James A. Jackson Community Service Award. He has received numerous recognition awards for outstanding service in the field of education. He is a member of Kappa Alpha Psi Fraternity.

He succeeded in helping to establish Eta Chi Chapter of Kappa Alpha Psi as the first Black Greek organization at the University of Alabama. He became the chapter's first official advisor.

His work experiences include teaching in the Tuscaloosa City Schools and Stillman College. He held administrative positions in the Macon County School System at Tuskegee, Alabama and St. Paul Public Schools, St. Paul, Minnesota. He recently retired from the Clayton County School System of Georgia.

After his retirement, he served as a volunteer tutor for adult males at the Atlanta Missions Center. Presently, he serves as a member and officer at the Quality Living Service Center for Seniors. He is a member of Elizabeth Baptist Church (Atlanta) where he serves in the ministries of Golden Years, Door Keepers and Hospitality. He is also a member of the Atlanta Inter-Alumni Council.

To recognize his decades of leadership, support and achievements in the areas of education and community service, Stillman College recently installed him into the Stillman College Education Hall of Fame.

Dr. Ashe is the author of four books: **UNDER THE MAGNOLIA TREE, POETIC EXPRESSIONS, MORNING TIME,** and **SOULFUL POETRY.** He is also the author, director and cast member of two comedy-spiritual plays, **"JUDGMENT DAY AT PEARLIE GATE COURT"** and **"SATAN TRIES TO SABOTAGE GOODNESS."**

Under The Magnolia Tree

Written by Richard D. Ashe

WITH MAJOR CONTRIBUTIONS BY

Annette Bing Austin

Frederick Blackburn

Robert E. Burns

Kim Eaton

Ed Enoch

Robert Heath

C. J. Johnson

Irma Blackburn McConner

Doris Hunter Metcalf

Marcia J. Millet

Wayne D. Mims

Pinkney Mosley

Woodrow M. Parker

Arlene Bell Peck

Floyd Phillips

Erma Roberts

Michelle A. Ross

Mary Sood

Haywood Strickland

Isaiah Sumbry

Vernon Swift

Jean Sykes

James Toombs

Bobbie Sellers West

Brooke Brandon White

BUILDERS OF THE MAGNOLIA LEGACY AND FOUNDATION

"When honeybees get together, they make honey.
When Stillmanites get together,
They make extraordinary things happen!"

R. D. Ashe

CHAPTER ONE

General Information

History

Stillman College, authorized by the General Assembly of the Presbyterian Church in the United States in 1875, held its first classes in the Fall of 1876. The Institution was headed by the Reverend Charles Allen Stillman, who presented an overture to the General Assembly of the Presbyterian Church in the United States asking the Church to establish a training school for black male ministers.

In the years that followed, the young school enlarged its academic program. In 1898, the school, now named Stillman Institute in honor of Dr. Stillman who died in 1985, moved to its present location in the western section of Tuscaloosa. In the next five decades, with the aid of the Church and under the able leadership first of Professor W. F. Osburn and later of Professor A. L. Jackson, the school grew in size and expanded in purpose. During these years, the school acquired its present campus tract of more than 100 acres.

The administration of Dr. Samuel Burney Hay extended from 1948 to 1965. In 1948 the name was changed to Stillman College, and the following year Stillman was expanded into a four-year college. Stillman graduated its first baccalaureate class in 1951. Seven buildings were constructed during his tenure.

Dr. Harold N. Stinson, the first African American to assume the presidency, served from 1967 to 1980. New programs designed to improve educational quality were instituted, and new facilities added included two men's residence halls, faculty apartments, a maintenance building, and a mathematics-science center.

Dr. Cordell Wynn, the fourth President, served from January 1982 through June 1997.

During his tenure, the appearance of the campus improved; Winsborough and John Knox Halls were renovated and the Marie Lundy Wynn Hall was erected. Under his leadership the enrollment grew beyond 1,000.

Dr. Ernest McNealey, the fifth President, assumed office in July 1997. He served until December, 2013. Dr. McNealey brought an emphasis on technology, connecting all buildings with fiber optic cable, providing computers and training for faculty and staff, and creating new laboratories for students. A stadium, a residence hall, a fine arts center, and a formal campus entrance have been constructed with several buildings renovated. *

On June 26, 2014, The Stillman College Board of Trustees announced the appointment of Dr. Peter E. Millet as the 6th President of Stillman College.

New and planned initiatives at the College by Dr. Millet include: 1) being a military friendly school, 2) allowing for the automatic admission of all graduates of Alabama Community Colleges, 3) offering free computer courses to the community, 4) giving K-12 students in Tuscaloosa free admission to home football games. Planned projects include: 1) constructing a Fitness/Exercise center for students, 2) offering graduate (M.A.) degrees, 3) scheduling "Alumni Days" at identified basketball and football games, 4) initiating an Alumni/Student mentoring project.

*Stillman College archives

STILLMAN AT A GLANCE
Established 1876

CHARACTER
Founded by Presbyterians in Alabama as a training school for black ministers. Today, Stillman is a top-tier, four-year co-educational, liberal arts college in the finest tradition.

MOTTO
Tradition, Excellence, Vision

COLORS
Vegas gold and navy

ENROLLMENT
Approximately 1,200 students

FACULTY
97 full-time and part-time faculty. Eighty-three percent of Stillman's full-time professors hold terminal (highest in field) degrees.

DEGREE PROGRAMS
Noted for its outstanding programs in the biological sciences, music and teacher education, Stillman offers 17 majors in the liberal arts that prepare students for most fields of graduate study and related careers. Pre-professional programs are available in law, medicine and ministry.

STUDENT/FACULTY RATIO
15:1, a ratio that ensures that every student receives personal attention.

CAMPUS LIFE
Stillman offers a wide range of academic, special interest, and performing arts clubs and organizations as well as organizations that address campus Christian life. The campus has chapters of eight national sororities and fraternities: Delta Sigma Theta, Alpha Kappa Alpha, Zeta Phi Beta, Sigma Gamma Rho, Kappa Alpha Psi, Phi Beta Sigma, Alpha Phi Alpha, and Omega Psi Phi.

ATHLETICS
Stillman is a member of NCAA Division II with intercollegiate teams for men in football, basketball, tennis, track, cross-country, and

baseball; and for women in basketball, tennis, track, cross country, softball and volleyball.

THE CAMPUS

A beautiful, 105 acre campus, located within walking distance of downtown Tuscaloosa. It is noted for stately magnolias, historic architecture and spacious, well-maintained grounds. The campus has 25 academic, administrative, residential, and recreational buildings.

AFFILIATIONS

The College Fund/UNCF and the Presbyterian Church (U.S.A.)

LOCATION

Tuscaloosa, Alabama, 52 miles southwest of Birmingham. Tuscaloosa is serviced by the Birmingham Shuttlesworth Airport, a drive of approximately one hour. Tuscaloosa is easily accessible by Amtrak rail and Greyhound Bus Lines.

ACCREDITATION

Stillman College is accredited by the Commission on Colleges of the Southern Association of Colleges and Schools to award baccalaureate degrees.

FINANCIAL AID

More than $10 million in federal financial aid and college scholarships are awarded annually.

Dean B. Brewster Hardy: The Man, Myth and Legend

(May 7, 1908-August 10, 1996)

By

Richard D. Ashe

As the case in most men of distinction, inevitably, there will be facts, myths and legendary stories that surround the individuals' life. So it is with Stillman's beloved and irreplaceable, the late, Dean B. B. Hardy.

Background Information

Dean Hardy was born in Eutaw, Alabama where he received his elementary and high school education. In 1931 he finished high school as valedictorian of his class. He enrolled in the Junior College Department at Stillman where he played end and guard on the football team, known as the Stillman "Tigers." He was salutatorian of the class in May, 1933.

He enrolled as a junior at Alabama State College in Montgomery and received his Bachelor of Science degree in Education in May, 1933. His first school assignment was as Assistant Teaching Principal in the Perry County Training School in Uniontown, Alabama. On October 17, 1944, Mr. Hardy received a special delivery letter from Professor A. L. Jackson, President of Stillman Institute, asking if he would return to his Alma Mater as Dean of the Junior College Department. He accepted the position and began his new work at Stillman on December 1, 1944.

After the close of Professor Jackson's period of leadership, (1929-47) and before the coming of Dr. Hay as president, the "Institute," then changed to "College" was carried on by Dr. A. R. Batchelor, then Secretary of Negro Work, who divided his time between the College and his office in Atlanta with Dean Hardy "holding things together,"

Over a period of years, Dean Hardy pursued further graduate study, first at Fisk University, where he was awarded his M. A. in Education in 1948; and finally came the degree of Ph.D in Educational Administration from Michigan State University in 1960. At a testimonial dinner, held in July 1973, Dean Hardy formally retired after 29 years as Dean, and was presented a watch by Dr. Harold N. Stinson, President of the College, as a tribute to his long years of service to the institution.

Myth

Upon this writer's arrival as a freshman at Stillman, one of the many stories that surfaced about the faculty was the Dean of the College, B. B. Hardy. The story alleges that one evening Dean Hardy had perched himself high upon one of the Magnolia tree's gigantic branch limbs. His intent was to view students who he felt were misbehaving and send them a letter of reprimand. The legendary story goes on to say that when a couple stopped under the magnolia tree, Dean Hardy tried to position himself on the limb to get a better view and identity of the couple.

At this point we are told that Dean Hardy lost his balance and fell from the tree, landing on the ground at the feet of the couple. Dean Hardy's first words were, "Well my fellow students." We are told that the startled and frightened students ran as fast as they could to their dormitory. Although this story continued to perpetuate itself years after the alleged incident, no one could ever give a specific time of the occurrence or identify the couple that was to have been under the magnolia tree when Dean Hardy fell. Nevertheless, this story has provided laughter among Stillmanites for decades.

Legacy

As for Dean Hardy, the man, no one can deny the true legacy of his contributions and what he meant to Stillman College. During my freshman year at Stillman, I recall several upperclassmen telling freshmen male students, "Be sure that you never disrespect a female student. If you do, expect to hear from Ms. Mckinney, the Dean of Students. If the "God Father," Dean Hardy handles the situation, expect him to give you a one way bus ticket, a comic book, a peanut butter and jelly sandwich, an apple and send you home." That warning let us know that Dean Hardy expected male students to always treat Stillman ladies with dignity and respect.

Dean Robert Heath, Stillman College archivist and Dean of Sheppard Library, remembers Dean Hardy as "a tall, handsome man who walked with "pep and purpose in his steps." "Dean Hardy was a talented and highly intelligent individual who made Stillman students feel proud." He also remembers how Dean Hardy worked tirelessly to ensure that Stillman met all requirements of the Southern Association of Colleges and Schools for accreditation.

Therefore, let the legacy of Dean Hardy include the statement that, "due to his love, tireless efforts and support for Stillman, the college became a first class accredited educational institution."

Dean Hardy and his wife, Eva Edwina were blessed with three children, Leon Brewster, Millard Lloyd and Leslie Sandra.

* (Biographical information from Stillman College Archives)

Cultivate a Spirit of Joy

By
Dr. Marcia J. Millet
First Lady of Stillman College

What an honor to serve as the sixth First Lady of Stillman College. As I reflect on the path that led me to this point in my life, I can truly say that God has ordered my steps. Growing up in North Carolina I can remember my church, teachers, neighbors and especially my mother instilling in me three important lessons: Love thy neighbor, be a person of integrity, and maintain a joyous and grateful spirit. These lessons are just as true today as they were when I was a child.

Maintaining a spirit of joy has not always been easy but with constant prayer and support from positive influences in my life, I have weathered many storms. I often find myself quietly watching and listening to others express their thoughts and fears about situations in their lives and ask, "Where is their joy?" A number of factors can lead people to lose their joy. For some it is related to concerns over life struggles such as those involving health, wealth, or self. Others may have a preoccupation with temporal issues such as physical appearance or status. Some have vocational, relational or family challenges that they are unable or unwilling to excise. Some are simply unwilling to forgive.

Regardless of the source of ones consternation, over the years, I have learned that joy is not determined by the amount of education an individual has, the amount of money one has amassed, the size of the house, the designer clothes one wears, or the materialistic things one has acquired. Rather joy is cultivated by helping others become the people they were destined to be. Joy is cultivated by the recognition that no one is a finished product, but rather clay on the Potter's wheel. Joy is cultivated by forgiving others as we wish to be forgiven ourselves. Joy is cultivated by standing up for what is right, even if one must stand alone. Joy is cultivated by realizing that everybody is somebody. Joy is cultivated by putting the needs of others before the needs of self.

As the sixth, First Lady of Stillman College it is my prayer that I will have the opportunity to serve, support and help cultivate within others a spirit of joy. I want to make a difference in the lives of the students, and the entire community. I believe joy is contagious and has the power to change the world. To cultivate a spirit of joy during your darkest moments, and when you feel most alone, remember, "Weeping may endure for a night, but joy cometh in the morning."

Dr. Marcia J. Millet is a 1984 graduate of Bennett College. She obtained the Masters Degree from The Ohio State University, and the Ed.D Degree from Tennesee State University.

The Power Of A Check

By
Erma Roberts

"Papa's gonna shoes your pretty little feet!"
"Mama's gonna glove your hands!"
"Sister's gonna kiss your pretty little cheeks!"

That was a song that my daddy sang to me as I sat on his knee until I was ten years old. Not only did he sing it to me, he sung this song to my five sisters too. I never heard anyone sing that song before my dad and I never heard anyone else sing it---ever.

That song had some very profound words and my dad spoke something into existence for me.

I lost my dad when I was ten years old. I remember everything about my daddy's death as if it was yesterday. You see, I was definitely a "daddy's girl" and when we lost him, our lives were devastated. My mother had to raise us as a single mom.

I grew up in a family of eight children---two boys and six girls. Early on, I was often identified as the "smart" little black girl by all that lived in the community. I really don't understand how I got labeled with that "smart" description, because I clearly was not the "smart" one in the pack. Whenever my mother thought I was being flippant or "too smart for my pants," she would address me as "Miss High and Mighty," which I took offense to.

My sixth grade teacher gave me another label. She referred to me as "The Queen of the Nile" and amazingly, I really believed that---not realizing that there never was a "Queen of the Nile". That tells you how "smart" I really was! I guess I can consider me being the *first!*

I have always loved oratoricals. I was always ready to stand before a crowd to speak. I always participated in school plays and skits and to this day, I enjoy making oral presentations.

I attended and graduated with honors (#5 in the class and in top ten percent) from an "all black historical" high school, George Perry Austin, at the tender age of sixteen. I was a member of Who's Who Among American High School Students, which both of these accomplishments were a *"first"* in my immediate family.

I had always wanted to attend Alabama State University to major in journalism. I got this idea from the only African-American female journalist I knew from watching the CBS evening news (I think she may have been the *first* African American female journalist).

Unfortunately, due to my financial situation upon graduating from high school, I was not able to enter college. Even though my family was dirt poor, we were never without the necessities of life. I went to work for a female apparel manufacturing company for one and one-half years (as a gusset girl) and saved as much money as possible. I, then, decided to attend what was commonly known as a technical school (now known as junior colleges and/or community colleges). I attended Hobson State Technical College for one year. I thoroughly enjoyed working with numbers (especially when it dealt with MONEY) and found a love for business, particularly accounting.

My journey to Stillman began in January, 1976, the year of its 100th anniversary. I guess I can say I was an integral part of the birthday present to Stillman, because, at that time, the freshman class was the largest class that ever entered Stillman in a spring semester. I don't remember the exact number, but I do remember that announcement being made.

I went to college to continue to receive my dad's social security! This is a true statement! I know it sounds rather "unintelligent", but it does warrant an explanation. When I entered Stillman, I had just completed my year at the junior college. I had no intentions of continuing my education. I just wanted to find a job and start earning money. During that time, if you were eighteen to twenty-two years of age, you could continue to receive your deceased parents' social security benefits as long as you were attending school and the check came in your name! I was not able to find a job immediately after the junior college; therefore, I had to make sure I had some type of income, so I, expeditiously, made sure I got into school so that my benefits would not be cancelled. I had applied to Alabama State University and Stillman and I went with the first one that accepted me. Time was of essence, because this all occurred during the Christmas break of 1975.

I never lived in what was known as the "freshmen's" dorm (Winnsborough). Because there were so many new students, I, along with several other girls, was lucky enough to be housed in Geneva Hall, which primarily housed sophomores. I ended up on the second floor in the first room on the green hall with three roommates (two of them from the same county I am from). For whatever reason(s), our room tended to be the "gathering place". I think it was primarily due to my roommates and I going home every single weekend and returning with our mothers' cooking --- enough to feed almost the whole dorm. Yes, my home girl and I went home every single weekend that first semester! Remember, it was the Centennial birthday, but we didn't care. All we were interested in was making it back to Linden, Alabama as soon as classes were over on Friday. We were so "green" or "wet behind the ears" (for lack of a better term or phrase), it didn't matter to us. We were packing up and going home --- celebrities and/ or free concerts on campus or not!

That first semester, the group of girls I associated closely with was penned with the name "Teenyboppers"! It was about seven or eight of us from various states that hung together. We had made that unspoken pact that we were going to look out for each other. The story on how we were indoctrinated into the social arena with that name requires too much detail to be shared in this setting, although it was really funny!

After my first semester, I didn't want to continue attending Stillman. I was determined to transfer to Alabama State. Even though I loved accounting, I still had a desire to pursue journalism. Two factors became pertinent in my decision to complete college and graduate from Stillman. As I mentioned before, I had attended a junior college and attained exceptional grades. After an assessment, Stillman accepted all of my coursework and I had enough hours to be classified as a sophomore. When I tried to transfer to Alabama State, they were not going to accept any of my hours; therefore, I was inclined to continue school at Stillman --- never with intentions of actually graduating.

Secondly, my long time friend had befriended a senior who was graduating that same semester. His family was unable to attend the graduation and he asked her to stay for the graduation and she, then, asked me to stay with her. So, I did. Upon attending the graduation, I saw how proud the graduates and their families were. It was overwhelming! I knew right then that I had to experience that same feeling --- especially since no one else in my immediate family had done so. Yes, I was the *first* in my immediate family to graduate from college! I had ions of cousins that had completed college, but my direct line had never had a college graduate.

During the summer of 1976, two or three significant things happened to encourage me to continue my education. I completed my first semester on the Dean's List. Secondly, and most important, I received a letter and an application for an academic scholarship from Stillman. Also, Hardees opened in Demopolis, Alabama. I was the first African-American cashier they hired. I know this seems like a small feat to address, but racial discrimination was still alive and well in the small towns of Marengo County. It was still very uncommon to see African-Americans in the front of a store during that time. My employment with Hardees was not very long, but you can see the pride in the African-Americans when they came in and saw a black face at the cash register.

Upon returning to school in the fall of 1976, I was informed that I was one of ten recipients of the Mary Failor Barrett Academic Scholarship! The scholarship was financially supported by a philanthropist in Texas who was a friend of descendants of Dr. Stillman. This was the best thing to happen to me in my whole life! All I had to do was maintain a "B" average and write the donor a letter regarding my status at the end of each year and that was the easiest part for me! I always enjoyed learning, so studying and making the grade was no problem for me.

I was the only member of the Teenyboppers that made the Dean's List. I will never forget what Yurlinda Johnson (a fellow Teenybopper) said to me after learning that I had made the Dean's List and received a scholarship. She congratulated me on my achievements and she vowed that she was going to do all that was within her powers to try harder to make better grades. She told me that I was her incentive to do better and she respected how I had performed so well that semester. Mind you, we did some partying at Stillman. In fact, it was at a party that we got crowned with that name, Teenybopper!

Getting educated socially and intellectually at Stillman gave me courage to do things that was practically unheard of in small town Linden, Alabama. The summer of 1977 was another significant time in my life for two unique reasons. Jobs were very hard to come by, especially if you were beyond high school. The high school kids were able to work in the summer job programs, but college students were not allowed to get those jobs. If you were above high school, you were on your own as for finding a job, which was few and far between.

I decided to do something courageous and different this particular summer. During this time, there was only one African-American working in the Marengo County Courthouse in an administrative or clerical position. It was the culture that only one was needed to meet the "quota" during those days. Even though in the very back of my mind, I felt they were not going to hire me because of my race, I made up my mind that I was going to go to the Courthouse and I was going to ask for a job "in the office". Not a janitor's job, but an "office" job. I had very good clerical skills and I knew how to present myself with confidence and poise. In other words I knew what to do and what to say to impress them that I could perform any administrative/clerical task that was presented to me. I did not tell anyone what I had planned because I didn't want to be embarrassed and joked for trying something like that. Well, I got the job!!! There, again, not just in my immediate family, but I was the very first African-American that was employed by the Tax Assessor's Office in Marengo County! I'm not really sure if I can say I got the job only because of my personal credentials. Ironically, it was my mother's natural culinary skills that gave the "powers to be" that final instinct to hire me. When they found out that I was Ella Mae's daughter, there was no hesitation in offering me a summer job. They knew all about my mother's good cooking and said if I can use the typewriter as well as my mother can cook, I have the job! That really was some big shoes to fill, but I was not about to let them down. Not only did I have to prove to them that I had skills, I had to prove to my mom that my education was paying off just as her cooking did!

The African-Americans could not believe it! They were so proud! It was something historical for my community! It was huge! Citizens (particularly the Blacks) would come in the courthouse just to look at that young "black" lady sitting at a desk in the County Courthouse!!! It was a monumental achievement and I accomplished something that was unthinkable at that time.

After I was hired, I encouraged other college students to go and apply for office jobs with any public facility in the county. I even gave them suggestions on how to answer certain questions to help them get the job. To my credit, my roommate and friend at the time also got hired with the County Health Department. She was also a "first" for the county and she is also a Stillman Grad. At that time, I really didn't realize that my actions were creating a movement in a positive direction for racial relations in Marengo County. My supervisor was very impressed with my work and my initiative and eagerness to learn. I didn't even have to apply for the job the next summer (1978). When I got out of school, I immediately went to work for them.

My second significant event that summer was being invited to pledge the greatest sorority ever---the sorority that is a *MOVEMENT----NOT A MONUMENT---DELTA SIGMA THETA SORORITY, INC.*!!! Again, no one in my <u>immediate</u> family had done this. There, again, I was the *first!*

There were many other revelations that occurred that impacted my time at Stillman. As I continued my education, I was affiliated with several organizations on campus which helped to educate me on a social level. I was really proud to become a member of the first sorority on Stillman's Campus, Delta Sigma Theta Sorority, Inc. and "Who's Who in American Colleges and Universities". I also ranked in the top 10% of my graduating class.

I completed my course work for a bachelor degree in Business in December 1978 and officially graduated on Mother's Day, May 1979. Again, I was the *first* in my <u>immediate </u>family to obtain an education beyond high school. It was the best gift I could have ever given my mother. When I left Stillman, Stillman owed me a refund! Something else that was unheard of during that time. It was enough to purchase my first genuine leather coat!

I often tell people that the three years I spent at Stillman College were the best years of my life! Often times, my husband feels offended by that statement-mainly, he says, because he and our children were not a part of my life during that time. Then I have to explain to him that my years at Stillman were the best years of my life <u>before</u> I met him. I consider those years as the best of my life because my experience at Stillman absolutely shaped my life. Stillman was the only single room dwelling that I have ever abided in, yet it was the place that provided me with more cultivation than any other place in my life.

My "firsts" did not end after my years at Stillman. I went on to be responsible for breaking more racial barriers throughout my employment. As I entered the job market, I was the first African American female to be employed in Human Resources by the Naheola Mill (a major employer in southwest Alabama). I went on to become the first and only African-American that served in the capacity of Finance Director Assistant/Cashier with the Naheola Mill.

I was not satisfied with myself educationally, so I continued my education at Florida Institute of Technology and received an MBA Degree in 1985; thus, becoming the *first* in my <u>immediate</u> family to earn an advanced degree.

I was the first and only African-American to be employed as a member of the Robert Bosch Power Tool Corporation "President's Cabinet" and the only African-American Auditor in its employ. I am also responsible for penning the name of "Patriots" for Linden High School mascot after the official integration of the schools. The origin of this is also a story for the dinner table. I had been taught 'negotiating skills" at Stillman and I conveyed those skills to a high school student on how to get the name accepted and it worked!

Other accomplishments I am very proud of are producing a booklet chronicling my family's genealogy, called "The Sankofa" Reunion. I am a fourth generation descendant of the infamous Glover-Rembert Clan from Rembert Hills, Alabama. A short conversation on my life is recorded and archived in the Smithsonian Institute through the Grios Project (which is a project recording African-American lives in the 21st century).

In many instances, people feel they have to make contributions that affect the entire world. I feel that if you can help one person on this earth in a positive way, you have done something to change the world. It only takes one person at a time. Although my successes may appear very small, I feel that I have encouraged, influenced, inspired and motivated many individuals to continue to elevate themselves physically, mentally, spiritually and financially. When I share my story, it gives individuals hope for their future.

Daddy did just what he said for the few years I shared with him.
He kept shoes on my feet and I am pretty sure he is proud of the grassy road that I took.
Mama gloved my hands until I was able to glove them myself.
Sister kissed my pretty little cheeks when I was discouraged
And an engineer became my man!

Today, I am married to Bruce Roberts, the engineer my daddy always told me I would marry! We have two sons, Maurice and Justin (Justin was the first African-American from Autauga County to graduate from Alabama School of Math and Science). My husband and I currently reside in Prattville, Alabama. I am currently employed with the City of Selma Finance Department, supervising Accounts Payable and Payroll and looking forward to retirement in three years!

I have lived throughout the southeast and have traveled throughout the U. S., Canada, Mexico and the Caribbean. My favorite hobbies are traveling, praise dancing, quilting and reading non-fiction.

Stillman College was the foundation for my life to emerge out of poverty. She was that self esteem booster. At 100 years old, she gave me the shot in the arm, the "oomph" that I needed to build self confidence. I shall forever be proud of the experience, the lifelong connections and grateful to the people that helped me along the way. I don't believe I could have had any better results at any other institution of learning!

I am a <u>Stillman</u> Tiger! You're gonna hear me roar!!!

Erma Roberts received the Bachelor of Science Degree from Stillman College, 1979 and the MBA Degree from Florida Institute of Technology.

Reflections on The Homegoing
of
Moses Kennedy Prewitt

Saturday, February 20, 2010
By
Haywood L. Strickland

Good Morning,

Pastor Bentley, to the family, to his special friend and companion, to those assembled here.

I come on behalf of the innumerable friends and colleagues of Moses Kennedy Prewitt as we celebrate his homegoing. My brother James and classmate Willie Davis asked me to call their names and pay their respects. The Wiley College Family who came to know Moses during his two visits to our campus asked that I would extend their deepest love and prayers for the family.

Our momentary sadness and sense of loss is tempered by the realization that Moses lived a quality life and touched and enriched the lives of so many people, and by the fact that he is now free of pain, hurt or worry.

I knew "Mose" for fifty years as a classmate, colleague, friend, and indeed, as a brother. When I first met him I was a junior in college and Moses joined our class after having served in the military. He was closer to my brother James then because they had been students together before "Mose" went in the service. He and James concocted many "potions" in the chemistry laboratory that would have attracted the "Revenooers" if they had known about it.

Moses was an outstanding basketball player. He was the center for the Stillman College Tigers. Those who saw him later in life could not imagine the poise and grace he exhibited on the court. But, Moses was slow - I do mean slow. He didn't believe in the fast break. He would take his time getting back down the court and getting into place. He would drive coaches Coleman and Whisenton (a.k.a."Whis") crazy. But, finally he would get in place and the play set up would begin.

Mose invented the sky hook-long before Jabbar made it famous (demonstration of his style, lean forward, then back, lean to the right, lean to the left--finally raising his leg as it pivoted--"swish, two points"). In one game, it took him so long that the referee called a foul on him. Whis jumped up shouting and asking, "What was the foul"? "What was the foul"? The referee shouted back, "Delay of game, Delay of game".

Moses was the "bright spot" on the basketball team. When the team traveled "Mose" sometimes would be commissioned to enter a white establishment and get food for the players. On one trip, they were stopped on one of these state highways late at night. An officer came to the car, shined his light in from person to person. Then he asked Mose, "Who are these boys you got in here with you"? Moses quickly answered-

"Just a few of my workers, I'm taking them back to the farm". The officer said, "Ok, but you be careful now."

After graduation, we lost contact as we went our separate ways and launched our professional careers. But we regained a relationship when he returned to Stillman as Director of Alumni Affairs in the 70s. Our friendship grew as Moses strived to develop a viable alumni program. (I served as president of the alumni association for some of those years). We spent innumerable hours planning and conducting meetings and developing or strengthening alumni chapters in the major cities and regions. Moses was responsible for getting the first grant to restore the Stillman House for alumni use. I appreciate Mrs. Wells'indication that a brick would be placed on the walkway to the house, but I believe that a room in the house should be dedicated to the life and service of Mr. Prewitt as well.

Moses loved Stillman and he gave her his very best. He didn't care who was president, vice president or whatever, he was going to serve Stillman and its students. Moses loved the students of Stillman. He was always willing to take time for them and support them. As a professional, Moses was dependable, dedicated, insightful and committed. Time did not matter when there was a task to be accomplished, a challenge to be met.

As a friend and brother to many, Moses was sensitive and caring. He was encouraging and facilitative and kind. He had a quick sense of humor and laughed often. He loved a good joke or tale. Moses, like all of us, had virtues and vices but his goodwill showed in the midst of all of them. He was strong, yet often quiet and silent. But when he spoke we all listened.

Finally Moses was a common man with common tastes. Don't get me wrong, he had sampled the best in life-had dined on caviar and sipped champagne, but a slab of ribs and a bottle of beer did him just fine. He did not suffer the pretentious gladly and in his enviable Archie Bunker fashion he would dismiss them with a flick of his hand and a "puuuh." He deflated many a human balloon.

This past year I saw the toll that the illness was taking on him, but he never complained. As soon as I came to town he would dismiss his pain and say let's go see "Kate" or "Dr. Wynn" or others who were sick. Then he, Jessica and I would have breakfast, lunch or dinner and go visit Mrs. Elouise and Norm.

I was blessed to be able to see him Saturday night and Sunday morning, for death stole him on Monday, February 15, 2010. Psalm 40:1 "I waited patiently for the Lord; and he inclined to me; and heard my cry." On February 15th, God heard Moses' cry. In my mind's eye, I can see the Holy Spirit delivering him to the gates of heaven. I see St. Peter reading the book. I hear him speak, "Moses, there are difficult and sinful things here to be true, but your great service to human kind wiped them out. You are forgiven. For you fed the hungry, clothed the naked and gave shelter to the shelterless. Welcome my child, come on in and make yourself comfortable." I can hear Moses say, "Thank you St. Peter, don't mind if I do." We will miss you Moses. May God greet you with a warm embrace!

Thank you so much.

Haywood L. Strickland,
President & CEO, Wiley College

Haywood L. Strickland received a BA degree from Stillman College in 1960 and the Ph.D from the University of Wisconsin.

The President Comes to the Rescue

(Dr. Samuel B. Hay Gives a Helping Hand)
By
Richard D. Ashe

During the summer of my sophomore year at Stillman College, I worked as a bellhop at the Assembly Inn in Montreat, North Carolina. My goal was to earn my first semester's tuition fee. My goal also was to work up to the last possible minute and hour until I had to get on the bus for Stillman.

I remember being very proud of accomplishing my goal. I even had enough to buy other items of choice throughout the semester. The saved funds consisted of dollar bills, and lots of coins that I had received from wages and tips. My determination to work as many hours on the payroll clock had gone exactly as planned.

However, when I started packing my belongings, I realized that all of my planning had not included taking time to convert the many bills and change into larger paper cash. Nevertheless, I stuffed my hard earned funds into a tin box container and placed it inside of my luggage. I bought a bus ticket and checked my luggage at the Trailways Bus Terminal for Tuscaloosa, Alabama.

When I arrived at my destination in Tuscaloosa, I remember stepping off the bus, sleepy and tired, but with a sense of self pride of what I had accomplished during the summer. I looked forward to starting my second year at Stillman with self confidence and determination. When the baggage handler at the Tuscaloosa bus station did not pull my luggage from the bus, I thought that this was quite odd. Other times when I traveled and checked my luggage with ticket clerks, my luggage arrived with me at my place of destination.

After my luggage failed to arrive that day, I filed a "Missing Luggage Report" with the Trailways Bus Office. I was very anxious and eager to get my luggage because my tuition fees for Stillman along with other personal items were inside and I desperately needed them. For three days, I waited and waited and waited for my luggage. On the fourth day I received a call from the bus station informing me that my luggage had arrived. I immediately went to the bus station to retrieve my luggage.

When the bus station attendant presented my luggage to me, I was astonished to see a rope tied around it to maintain the items inside. My luggage had been pried open by someone. After examining my luggage, I discovered that the tin money box was missing along with other items that were inside of my luggage. Immediately, I complained to the bus station attendant and filed another report, hoping that my tuition fees and other personal items would be returned. A week later I received a formal letter from the Trailways Bus Company declining to accept responsibility for the missing money and other items that I reported missing.

The Trailways' letter was not only disappointing to me, but I was mentally distraught at the notion of not having first semester funds to pay Stillman College. I blamed myself for my failure to take care of those "precious funds." My haste to catch the bus on time back to Stillman; and not converting the dollar bills and change to larger currency was my fault. I also blamed myself for being so naïve to think that baggage handlers at bus stations were very honest and trustworthy with other people's property. The fact of the matter is, I made it easy for a dishonest person to examine my baggage due to the sound that came from the money box that was tucked away inside of my luggage.

Desperately, I made my way to the Office of the President of Stillman College, Dr. Samuel B. Hay. After explaining my ordeal to Dr. Hay, I pleaded with him not to send me home because I didn't have the money. Dr. Hay looked at me with a stern look in his eyes and said, "Mr. Ashe, we would never think of sending you home because you don't have the money."

Dr. Hay then called the Bursar, Mr.Burt Vardeman into his office and asked me to explain my circumstances to him. After explaining my situation to Mr. Varderman, Dr. Hay said, "Burt, take care of this for me."

Dr. Hay's intervention on my behalf led to my receiving help from a Presbyterian Church donor from Tennessee. A couple of weeks later, I wrote a thank you letter to the donor for supporting me during my desperate need for peace of mind and financial assistance.

For what Dr. Hay had done for me, he became my number one hero. I also thanked God for leading me to Dr. Hay's office.

Strategies That Prevent College Failure

By
Richard D. Ashe

Over the years, this author had the privilege to observe the study habits of many students. The students observed were high school or college students. During this period of observation, I was either a student or teacher.

As I recall, my school advisors or counselors gave students important clues as to how to become a successful college student. However, my observations of many students who failed to become successful college students probably failed to implement some of the basic strategies for college success. Therefore, this author believes that if high school or college students implement the strategies below, they will become strong academic achievers.

1. **Have clear goals.** Write down the specific goals that you wish to achieve. The goals should be attainable and measurable. As a first step in defining what you wish to achieve, ask yourself the following questions:

    A. What are my goals and what do I want to accomplish?

    B. What essential materials and procedures must I utilize to achieve my goals?

2. **Develop a strategic plan of action.** After developing a plan of action, implement your action plans.

3. **Sitting areas in the classroom.** Choosing to sit in the first three rows is an indication of your intention to grasp all of the information that will be offered. Back row sitters are generally there to meet course requirements.

4. **Note taking.** Be sure to take accurate notes. Developing a short hand scheme for words will be helpful.

5. **Review notes**. A habit of reviewing class notes at least every other day will allow you to retain pertinent and factual information about the subject matter.

6. **Notebooks.** Have a notebook for each course. Having course notes in the same notebook can lead to uncertainty and confusion. It is easier to organize materials in loose leaf notebooks.

7. **Become a member of a subject matter study group.** Study groups allow members to exchange information and

ideas about course contents. Life long friendship may also develop.

8. **Allow adequate planning time to study for tests.** Do not wait until two or three hours before a test to begin studying. A two or three week head start will likely lead to very satisfying results. I don't know who to contribute this quote to, but I like it. "Prior planning prevents poor performance."

9. **Prioritize your time wisely.** You will find that time is invaluable. It is a precious resource that only you can control. The urge to socialize and go partying will be tempting throughout the week. A failure to manage this urge will lead to un -pleasant consequences.

10. **Choosing friends.** My parents instilled in me at an early age that, "you are judged by the company that you choose." Try to select friends who have similar goals and aspirations that you have. Respect everyone, but be careful who you choose as your friends.

11. **Healthy eating habits.** We live in a society where food is practically available whenever we choose to eat. Advertisements are designed to lure you to eat their product regardless of side affects on the body. What you choose to eat will ultimately determine how well you live. Get familiar with literature that encourages healthy diets.

12. **Get proper rest.** There's an old cliché that says, "You can't romp with the owls at night and expect to soar with the eagles in the morning." The obvious lesson in that statement

is the persuasion to get adequate sleep and rest. This is essential if one expects to perform at a high level.

13. **Get to know your teachers.** Put forth an effort to get to know your teachers and let your teachers know you. Have periodic office visits to consult with your teachers for clarifications, feedback, and expectations.

14. **Check with academic advisors.** Periodically check with an academic advisor to monitor your academic progress.

15. **Establish good personal hygiene.** Having positive hygiene habits will help to establish a healthy lifestyle.

16. **Choose a compatible roommate.** It may not always be possible to select your roommates. However, it's ideal when like minded interests are placed together. Try to refrain from aligning yourself with individuals whose purpose is secondary to academic achievement.

17. **Develop networking skills.** Developing networking skills is important. Making contact with influential individuals who work in your career field will help to broaden your knowledge base for future references.

18. **Develop leadership skills.** Develop leadership skills in areas of interest by joining groups that will allow you to develop leadership skills.

19. **Respect ideas and skill level of others.** Regardless of another's philosophy, race, or intellectual ability, treat them with dignity and respect.

20. **Handling disrespectful comments.** Part of learning to become successful is knowing how to handle indirect or direct disrespectful comments. Remember, "It's not so much about the disrespect that you receive, but how you choose to respond to the disrespect."

21. **Don't be a class clown if you are not the class clown.** I've been told that laughter is good for the soul. However, unless you are studying to be a professional comedian, leave the jokes outside of the classroom. Refrain from getting a reputation for not being serious about your academic intentions.

22. **Arrange to have a mentor.** Seek to have a mentor who will give advice about your career objectives; someone to help you to keep focused. A minister, social worker, or an upper class big brother or sister can serve this purpose.

23. **Don't let Alcohol or Dope destroy your Hope.** This author has no intention of trying to force my values on anyone. My views are only my views. At an early age, I decided that I would control whatever goes inside of my body; and that I would not become addicted to any substance that could control me. A lack of discipline or moderation on anything will eventually cause an imbalance on everything.

24. **Develop a time schedule.** A time schedule will allow you to see how you spend your time during a typical day, week or month. A time schedule will also allow you to prioritize goals, objectives and make necessary adjustments for studying.

25. **Take time to meditate.** Take at least 15 minutes each day to meditate. There are many advantages to daily meditation. Implement it into your schedule.

26. **Study for each class period.** The professor may call on you to respond to the assigned subject matter to be discussed. There's also the possibility of a pop quiz.

27. **Always be punctual.** Don't allow tardiness to become a part of your character or reputation. Being punctual is a characteristic that's worthy of having.

28. **Don't give up because it's hard.** Life is full of ups and downs and many mountains to climb.

29. **Stick to difficult tasks.** Learning to persevere is an essential lifelong skill to have.

30. **Utilize your talents.** Your task is to make the very best use of the talents that God has given you.

The Joy and Necessity of Giving Back to HBCU Schools

By

Richard D. Ashe

I wish to commend the consistent contributors of Historical Black Colleges and University alumni who are diligent in their efforts to give financial support to their alma mater. I submit to you that there is no greater feeling of self satisfaction than to give so that others will have an opportunity to succeed.

It has been said many times that "successful achievers do not make it by themselves. They receive help from the labor and sacrifice of others." For decades, HBCU institutions have survived and thrived due to the generosity of alumni, friends, federal and state grants, along with corporate gifts.

However, due to the recent recession and cutbacks in gifts along with federal and state assistance, HBCU schools have been dealt a huge financial blow. This has caused the downsizing of essential services that these schools offer. This is why it is not only important for HBCU alumni to "step up to the plate," but it is also appropriate for them to increase their financial giving. Concerted efforts must also be made to get non contributing alumni to begin to give.

James Lemon, a graduate of North Carolina A&T State University states: "HBCUs have to face the reality that this is a competitive market in a global economy and public and private resources are scarce. Therefore, HBCUs must develop survival strategies to enhance their position in the educational arena. These strategies should include the following: 1) develop academic enhancement programs for underachieving minority students at the elementary and secondary school level as a community service for potential applicants; 2) foster relationships with academic successful minority high school students as a source to improve the academic atmosphere and raise student selectivity; 3) develop and implement a plan to substantially increase the school's endowment through innovative and creative fundraising methods; and 4) recruit faculty and staff that can generate research contracts and/or grants and provide profitable consultancy services to business and industry.

One essential and overlooked fundraising method is the creation of an alumni relations program which promotes alumni giving. Many HBCUs tend to minimize this important avenue of cash flow because of their marginal and/limited activities with the alumni. A broad and comprehensive alumni relations program helps establish a culture of giving that is vital to the success and sustainability of an institution. In other words, HBCUs must be proactive because the "forty acres and a mule" is not forthcoming.

Adeyemi Toure, the father of a son who attends Howard University declares: "HBCUs have remained the lifeline to "falling in love with the process of education and development!" These institutions remain the repository of our past, present and future. As such, they affirm us in the world. Let's be clear, after our faith-based institutions, HBCUs were/are the single most powerful transformative organizing tool for African-American culture. Most of our great personalities of color (too many to name here) were recipients of an HBCU socialization process. In the absence of a nurturing and too often, brutal dominant culture through Jim Crowism and segregation policies, our legacy and heritage of struggle found sanctuary, educational guidance and training administered by HBCUs. As our ancestors taught, struggle is natural and fundamental to life. When that principle is fully practiced and understood, the ensuing process grounds us in personal development.

Our elder Fannie Lou Hamer, taught us to "Never forget where you came from and always give praise to the bridge that brought us..." Alumni of HBCUs should remember that memory is sacred, and what's more precious and sacred than supporting our own to ensure a collective and victorious future!

City Councilman, Billy S. Martin of Marion, N. C. and a graduate of Winston-Salem State University asserts: "Predominately Black colleges and universities have produced individuals who have made significant contributions to the building of this great nation we call America. Graduates have taught, inspired and encouraged many of our great leaders down through the years. Education has been the conduit through which values, conscience, pride and loyalty emerged. Never has so many done so much with so little."

Sherrilyn Ifill, President and DirectorCounsel of the NAACP Legal Defense Fund says: "We should all make an effort to help ameliorate the financial catastrophe faced by college students at HBCUs as a result of the new PLUS loan standards."...

"No student should be denied a college education because of an inability to pay, especially because college education is directly tied to economic opportunity and advancement."

These compelling pleas and reasons for HBCU support is an indication as to why it is extremely important for HBCU graduates to stay involved and give back to their alma mater. It is sad and unfortunate that too many alumni are on the sideline being comfortable and complacent with not giving financial support to their school. I am hopeful that this article will appeal to the hearts and minds of these non-contributing HBCU graduates.

HBCU alumni must never allow our institutions to stop providing the extraordinary service that they make available for its students and communities. A part of that extraordinary service that HBCU institutions provide is the caring, nurturing and tutoring that students receive. The development of leadership skills at HBCUs is quite prevalent. Documented studies have concluded that the majority of African American leaders graduated from HBCU institutions.

Accordingly, I strongly beseech HBCU alumni to rededicate yourselves to the task of assisting with the dreams and aspirations of present and future generations of students at your respective school. Let each of us insure that our legacy will not only show that we attended an HBCU school, but it also shows that we gave back to our alma mater to help continue our school's efforts to provide a quality education for its enrollees.

I urge HBCU non-contributing graduates to wake up from the dark and sleepy shadows of complacency and walk into the bright sunshine with HBCU contributors. I am convinced that you will experience the delightful joy of knowing that your efforts helped others to have an opportunity to benefit from a quality college experience.

Let there be no doubt that I do not wish for my comments regarding non-contributing HBCU graduates be construed as a condemnation of them. I realize that circumstances and situations are not the same for everyone. My appeal is especially for HBCU alumni who have been blessed and have the financial resources to become a financial blessing to their alma mater's mission.

Therefore, I wish to reemphasize that all HBCU graduates should come to the realization that their successful achievement of obtaining a degree was not solely through their efforts alone. Somebody, somewhere, contributed in some form or another to their success. I hold the position that financial giving is an appropriate and essential way to say to your alma mater: "Thank you for what you did for me; and for carrying on the legacy of our HBCU forefathers."

Needless to say, because of the economy and recession, many HBCU schools will be forced to reevaluate the way they appeal to alumni and other sources for contributions. A failure to do so will only produce negative results. For decades HBCU institutions have done a remarkable job with preparing its students to become productive citizens and leaders. In order to continue this legacy, HBCU schools and its graduates must begin to seek new ways to strengthen its partnership with each other. If they heed this challenge, amazing results will likely occur on a grander scale.

If we embrace and harness the ideas offered in this article for HBCU financial support, we all will share and reap the dividends from our collective efforts.

Stillman
Beauty
Queens

Yesteryear Campus Queens

UNDER AND AROUND THE MAGNOLIA TREE

Take time to check your educational attitude,
for ultimately it will determine your life's altitude.

R. D. Ashe

CHAPTER TWO

Under and Around the Magnolia Tree

Have You Been Magnoliatized?

By

Richard D. Ashe

This author has no intention of dwelling on the rich history of the magnolia tree other than to say it is named after a French botanist, Pierre Magnol. However, I will attempt to give a very small synopsis of how one gigantic magnolia tree at Stillman College has become a symbol of strength, beauty, affection and warm memories to thousands of Stillman College alumni.

Upon my arrival at Stillman decades ago, the campus was graced with four magnolia trees. Today, three magnolia trees still stand. Over the years one magnolia tree became a victim of severe weather storms and campus refurbishing.

The largest magnolia tree stands at the center of the campus lawn. It also stands at the edge of a sidewalk shaped fork that allows walkers to reach other areas of the campus. For years, this gigantic magnolia tree was the focal point and destination for late evening strolls by couples.

This magnolia tree could easily accommodate the private standing space of at least six couples. Many students have been teased about "spending more time under the magnolia motel than inside of the classroom." Needless to say, numerous couples found standing or sitting under the magnolia tree to be refreshing and relaxing.

Just mentioning the magnolia tree to Stillman alums will likely get a reaction of a smile, grin, grunt, giggle, or raised eyebrows. On the other hand, a facial expression of sadness may also be displayed. It is likely that- that expression comes about because they didn't get the opportunity to get escorted and be "magnoliatized" by the beautiful gigantic tree.

Legendary stories say, to become "magnoliatized" by the tree, **a couple must stand, embrace and kiss under the tree's gigantic branches.** Upon completing this ritual, the tree grants the couple, individual luck, good fortune and good health. It has also been said over and over again that once couples have been magnoliatized, they always walk away grinning, grunting or giggling.

So my fellow alums, if you didn't have an opportunity to get "magnoliatized" while you were a student at Stillman, I urge you to take advantage of your next visit to the campus for homecoming, athletic events or for other occasions and get it done. With your spouse or significant other, **Just do it!** You will be glad that you have finally become **"magnoliatized."**

If that Magnolia Tree Could Talk

By

Richard D. Ashe

Stillman's famous, giant magnolia tree stands a few yards outside of Sheppard Library. It has become Stillman's insignia. It has appeared on the covers of the college's major print outs, publications and correspondence. Over the years this giant and magnificent tree has stood and survived devastating storms that affected the city of Tuscaloosa and the campus of Stillman College.

For decades, I've heard Stillman alumni say, "If that magnolia tree could talk, it would have a lot to say." As I go into the "theatre of my mind," I believe if it were possible for the magnolia tree to talk, it might say to students and alumni, "Just like you, I've experienced and witnessed lots of good times at Stillman. Not all of my days have been bright and sunny. There were days when dark clouds hung over my head.

I've experienced deafening sounds of thunder; the brilliant bursts of lightening; and the howling winds of tornado rain. I've also experienced many hot and steamy days. I've suffered through numerous bone chilling and freezing days as well. There were days when my future and survival were uncertain. I've also witnessed numerous and unexpected changes at Stillman. Never the less, I'm still standing tall to display my strength and beauty during the summer, winter, spring and fall.

For decades, my enormous branches and powerful limbs extended wide, high and low to the ground. After an extreme makeover by tree trimming surgeons, I no longer look the same. I no longer draw couples who wish to embrace, hold hands and have a few moments of privacy. However, I now draw large crowds for special occasions such as concerts and graduation commencements.

I'm pleased that for nearly one hundred and fifty years, thousands of couples stopped under my gigantic branches to discuss issues of their concern. I've seen tears of joy, relationships repaired, terminated and destroyed. I've observed many faces that showed surprise, disappointment, confusion, anger, joy and happiness. I've heard laughter, sounds of weeping and sighs of pleasurable fulfillment.

Through it all, I remain standing tall as a beacon of light, hope, dreams and aspirations. I stand tall as a symbol of perseverance, achievement and high standards for past, present and future Stillmanites everywhere."

The magnolia tree might also say, "Always remember to support your alma mater, through your time, talents and resources. Be proud of your school and always be a proud Stillmanite."

Who Would Have Ever Thought It

BY

Arlene Bell Peck

"Precious memories...how they do linger...how they do ever flood my soul..."

Memories of my time at Stillman continue to captivate my thoughts of the best four years of my life. The absolute value of a college education lies in **"learning how to learn."** This is an understatement to say the least. The great test comes when the schooling is over. We have the opportunity to discover whether the learning took... that is, can we navigate the unsuspecting **"yellow brick road?"** In the pursuit of an education one expects to achieve academic success when self discipline and hard work are applied. That's a given. My Stillman experience was so much more. A myriad of challenging, as well as loving and precious memories continue to flood my innermost being as I reflect on those remarkable years which could have been

53

referred to as **"the best of times and the worst of times."** This may sound a bit cynical to some, but not so much.

A place for social revolution…Who would have ever thought that I would have the nerve to sit in the "wrong" seat on the bus in Tuscaloosa, Alabama in the 1950's?

1956 was a time of heightened racial unrest and impending social revolution, when many parents were afraid to send their children away from home to college or anywhere else. As a young, naïve, sixteen year old from Birmingham, Alabama, aware of the need for social change, I just couldn't wait for the end of my senior year to arrive. I would graduate from high school and go to college to make my mark on the world. I was determined that I could somehow effect change that would make the world a better place than it had been for my parents and ancestors and a place where future generations would not have to face the injustices that we experienced. I had always been taught by my family and teachers throughout my life that a good education was the key and Stillman was going to let me fulfill my dream.

So, in the fall of 1956 when I arrived at Stillman to begin charting the course for my journey, my future evolved in a way that I could never have imagined in my wildest dreams. I began to get a sense of how right it felt to get to know people from other races, backgrounds and cultures. This heightened my desire to somehow effect change. I actually began to think that I could somehow put an end to segregation for one thing. There was one time when I was nearly put off a city bus because I took a seat in front of the sign that designated that all "colored" should sit **behind** the sign. The only open seat when I boarded the bus just happened to be in front of the sign. I was very conscious of the risk, but I thought I would take my chances and "try" the system.

The bus driver was very careful to drive on to the next stop until someone sitting in the back of the bus got off. He then turned and ordered me to either move to the rear or get off the bus. I remember thinking that I had let my people down. To this day, I don't recall that I ever breathed a word about the incident when I finally got back to campus, for fear of getting sent home. But from that experience I learned that change takes **planning** and **community.** By being a student at Stillman I was in the process of **learning how to learn.** I am so glad that change eventually came, but had I made a difference? Might just one person on that bus have been encouraged by or learned anything from that incident? If so, Stillman and God get the credit.

A place with fringe benefits ...who would have ever thought that Stillman also gives birth to "ODD COUPLES" like Steve and me, for instance? This particular happenstance could only have taken place at Stillman. They say, "opposites attract," right? Well, it's true. Our personalities are as different as night and day. Steve is the true introvert and eternal pessimist. And me, I'm a true extrovert and eternal optimist. Yes, this was a challenging time "high above the Warrior's waters ...," but the best part is that Stillman is where Steve and I met and fell in love. Little did either of us know at the time that we would indeed travel down a very long, blessed, eventful and challenging **"yellow brick road"** together. Yet, that is just what we are actually still doing after nearly fifty-three years of marriage and yes...we still are **"THE ODD COUPLE"** for sure. But we compliment each other well and this has given special meaning to **"learning how to learn."** To think that our life together began at Stillman during that second week of Freshman Orientation in 1956 remains mind-boggling to this day. Our journey has, as most, been challenging, but what we **learned how to learn** at Stillman has helped us rise to the challenge.

One of the most embarrassing and scary experiences we still laugh about is when each of us was called to the office of the Dean of Students for being caught courting "under the magnolia tree" one night after leaving the library. The funny thing is that it was a long time before either of us knew that the other had been summoned to Dean McKinney's office. One really had to have known Dean McKinney to appreciate the humor in this story. In her smug, very proper and serious manner she reprimanded us for "lingering" under the Magnolia tree. As she stared at me from behind her desk, I trembled deep down inside in fear that surely she was about to tell me that I was being expelled because my bill wasn't paid (daddy just didn't have the fifty dollars to pay each quarter) or that I had done something that merited my expulsion from school. Either scenario would mean that I would be thoroughly humiliated and embarrassed and in serious trouble. I can still hear her very somber, stern words as she said to me, "Miss Bell, do you not know that students are expected to be in transient on the campus at night?" (In other words she meant that we were not supposed to be standing still, but moving ... placing one foot in front of the other and going somewhere.)

I was a little confused for a few minutes and then I remembered that just the night before, Miss Tuson, the then head librarian, had walked past Steve and me while we were "paused" under the giant, beautiful **magnolia tree** that still graces the entrance of Shepherd Library to this day. She even greeted us as she strolled by. I remembered that she headed directly over to Winsborough Hall, though we really did not give it much thought at the time. Not too much time passed

56

before Steve walked me to the dorm and we said our goodnight and he made his way to Knox Hall where he lived. Aha! I thought. Miss Tuson must have reported seeing us "under the magnolia tree" to the house mother, Ms. Harvey, and perhaps then to Dean McKinney. The irony is that the library's brilliant porch light illuminated the entire walkway in front of the library as bright as day. Needless to say, that experience was enough to put the fear of God in me about pausing under the magnolia tree, any other tree, nor anywhere else on the campus at night or hardly any other time with Steve or with anyone else.

To be certain however, were it not for my time at Stillman I may never have met and married Steve, nor would we have the most awesome, remarkable and loving family in the world. In fact I am sure of it!

It is because of all those "who would ever have thought its?" that retrospectively I now pinch myself and wonder, "Was that actually me?" Memories of those exciting years and what God and Steve and I have produced as a result of our time **"Under the Magnolia Tree,"** are permanently etched in the recesses of my heart, mind and soul. **Mind-boggling** for sure, but like Maya Angelou, **"I wouldn't take nothing for my journey now."**

Arlene Bell Peck, Class of 1960 received a Bachelor degree from Stillman College and a Masters Degree from the University of Tennessee. She is enrolled in the Doctoral Program at the University of Tennessee.

Interview with Former "Miss Stillman"

Name: Bobbie Sellers West   **Year as "Miss Stillman":** 1970-71

What is your favorite memory while serving as "Miss Stillman"?

By far, my favorite memory of myself as "Miss Stillman, 1970-71 was my coronation. It was by far the most magical thing that had happened to me in my life! I floated around in a dream. All of the students were so supportive of me.

My Sorors of Delta Sigma Theta Sorority, Inc., Epsilon Eta Chapter were especially helpful to me. I did not have a thing of my own to wear and could not afford to go shopping. One Soror wrote a relative in Memphis and asked to allow me to wear her beautiful beaded gown for the coronation, and the relative was more than happy to help. She sent the gown to the school in ample time before the coronation ceremony. It was a perfect fit. Other Sorors made sure that my hair and make-up were regal, and that I had all of the accessories-earrings, bracelet, etc. I needed to look my best. On top of all of that, I succeeded a Soror as "Miss Stillman" who crowned me as her Successor. She, Marsha Webb, had also been my personal "Big Sister" when I pledged the Sorority.

During the coronation, I danced with Stillman President Dr. Harold Stinson. He was a smooth dancer and very understanding that I was nervous. He carried on a friendly conversation while we were on the floor to help me relax, and it worked. I also danced with Charles Lett, who represented the Student Government Association, and he also was very helpful in my becoming comfortable during the evening.

As a gift from the school, I received a beautiful gold musical jewelry box, which I have to this day. And the music still plays and the ballerina still dances.

In what ways did serving as "Miss Stillman" influence your life over the years"?

Serving as "Miss Stillman, 1970-71" opened up a whole new world for me. I gained confidence that I could excel at whatever my hands undertook. I became more poised in my conversations and dealing with all kinds of people. It taught me how to be a servant without being a doormat, and how to step out on faith for what I wanted in life. I learned that nothing beats a failure but a try. I became more outgoing and interested in things outside my everyday surrounding.

My time as "Miss Stillman" also increased my understanding of people and made me curious to meet people of other cultures. I think my time as "Miss Stillman" influenced me to venture from the South for a time and even travel overseas. I spent a year in Seoul, South Korea, after serving as Miss Stillman, and spent a week in Japan. I went on to graduate school after that at Northern Illinois University in DeKalb, Illinois, and then started a 34-year career with the Federal Government, first in Chicago, Illinois, and then in Atlanta, Georgia. I truly believe that serving as "Miss Stillman" opened my eyes to new possibilities in life.

What memories of Stillman readily come to mind when you think of Stillman?

I loved going to the dances in the Student Center on Friday nights. I had never been one to hit the dance floor before coming to Stillman, but those dances gave me an opportunity to meet and mingle with schoolmates that I did not see on a regular basis because we did not have classes together. Also, most of us were not great dancers, so everybody fit right in. Nobody cared what you looked like on the dance floor. We were just there to enjoy the music, the camaraderie, and the atmosphere.

I also loved sitting under the magnolia trees between classes in the spring time. The trees provided shade from the sun and a cool, relaxing breeze as well as an opportunity to people watch and "meet and greet." Stillman was a friendly, close-knit campus and we all knew each other. When one of us sat under the magnolia trees, someone else always came by to join you and make sitting and relaxing even more enjoyable.

I loved the students and faculty at Stillman. Everyone was so friendly and helpful. Everyone on campus made life worthwhile.

What teachers at Stillman inspired you?

English was one of my favorite subjects, and one of the English teachers who inspired me most was Miss Land. I can't recall her first name but she told the class on the very first day that the only person who made an "A" in her class was the writer of the text. I found that statement interesting, challenging, and inspiring, as I wanted to see if I could be as good as the writer of the text by the end of the semester. I studied hard for the class and was present for every class session. I earned an "A" in Miss Land's class.

Armondo and Estifana Martinez were the Spanish teachers when I was a student at Stillman. Their class was very "conversational" and dedicated to making learning to speak Spanish fun. Whenever you ran into them on campus, they carried on a conversation with you by asking questions in Spanish and you were expected to respond in Spanish. They were very patient with us students and helped us a great deal to learn conversational Spanish.

Reverend Charles Williams was the Pastor at Brown Memorial Presbyterian Church on Stillman's campus and also the Religion teacher. He had a great sense of humor, which made learning Religion more interesting. Although I was never Presbyterian, I attended services at Brown Memorial every Sunday just to hear Reverend Williams preach an inspiring sermon. He closed each service with a Bible passage that came to be my favorite Scripture:

"The Lord bless you and keeps you.
The Lord cause His face to shine upon
you and be gracious unto you.
The Lord lift up His countenance upon you and give you peace."
Numbers 6:24-26 (King James Version)

What additional comments would you like to make as a former "Miss Stillman"?

It was a wonderful, "fairy-tale" experience! To this day, nothing compares to it ...not even my wedding day. Although times have changed and "Miss Stillman's" responsibilities are more numerous, I would challenge any young woman to seek the opportunity. It is life-changing. It is an opportunity to represent the school at different functions and build lasting relationships. It provides an opportunity to serve the school as a good will ambassador of sorts. It builds confidence and poise. It's just life-changing.

Bobbie Sellers West, Class of 1971 also received a Master of Arts degree from Northern Illinois University

A Mountaineer Enrolls
at Stillman College

By
Richard D. Ashe

Upon graduating from Mountain View High School in Marion, North Carolina, I decided to accept a job that would take me further up into the "Blue Ridge Mountains." The job that I accepted was summer employment at the Assembly Inn (Hotel) in Montreat, N. C. For the most part, Montreat was a center for Presbyterian Church conferences. It was also the location of Montreat College as well as a summer home for many wealthy Presbyterians who owned luxury summer Cottages.

My job at the Assembly Inn as a bell hop was basically an extension of the same kind that I held at Hotel James after school hours. During my first week of employment in Montreat, I met a young minister who recently graduated from Stillman College. His name was Isaac Crosby. Isaac was the Director of the Recreational Center. During the course of the summer, we became friends. He loved sports and so did I. We enjoyed and admired each other's competitive spirit. I couldn't help but to think that if Isaac liked my competitiveness, he would have been in awe of my older brothers, Benny and Leonard. The two of them were high school sport stars in baseball and basketball.

Eventually, Isaac asked me about my career goals. I informed him that at the conclusion of my summer job at the Assembly Inn, I planned to join the military just as my oldest brother, Clifton had done. He then showed me several Stillman College year books. He pointed out sports programs that surely got my attention. He said that Stillman was a small Presbyterian school with an outstanding faculty. He stressed that Stillman was unique because everyone was considered a family member. I let Isaac know that under no circumstances was I going to college because college was for the smart and super intellectuals.

To appease my new friend Isaac, the two of us constructed a letter to Stillman College requesting an application. Several days later the application arrived. I had no intention of filling out the form and submitting it. However, at Isaac's insistence, the two of us filled it out and mailed the necessary information to Stillman. Although several weeks went by, I thought nothing else about the application. My mind was set on my original goals prior to meeting Isaac Crosby which was to join the military at the conclusion of my summer job.

After another couple of weeks, I received a letter from Stillman. However, I chose to ignore it. On the other hand, Isaac continued to ask me if I had heard from Stillman regarding my application. I told him that I received something in the mail and when I have time, I would let him know the nature of its contents. After work the next day, I took the letter by the Recreational Center where Isaac worked. When I opened the letter, we saw: "Congratulation, you have been accepted to enroll at Stillman College." Isaac began to jump for joy. He congratulated me and then began to tell everyone he knew that I had been accepted at Stillman College. They too were excited and congratulated me. I then began to realize that being accepted to college must be a "**big mothering deal.**"

Isaac's enthusiasm did not stop there. He contacted Ms. Margaret Davis, a Spanish teacher at Stillman and got her to pay for the cost of my books for the year. Then the two of us drove to my hometown of Marion and asked my sister, Gertrude Ashe Forney if she would assist in paying my tuition. Immediately, she said "Yes." A financial strategy to defray the tuition obligation would prove to be successful. I would obtain a work-study job on campus; obtain a job during the summer months to fulfill the first semester expenses; and my sister, Gertrude would assist with the second semester tuition costs.

Although I had prepared myself mentally to go into the military, I had not prepared myself for the life of a college student. This mountaineer had never stepped foot onto a college campus before other than Montreat where I worked. I was literally frightened of having to leave the comfortable confines of my mountain life style. I came to realize that I spoke the dialect of the region and my community. However, when I spoke, the subject of my sentences never agreed with the verbs. Not only that, I had developed a habit of not being able to look adults directly in their face or eyes. I always looked past them or looked downward. This habit came about because I had not developed self confidence in my ability to verbalize and speak grammatically correct.

Although somewhat skeptical of my ability to be successful at the college level, I prepared myself to leave my mountain surroundings for the journey to Stillman College.

As I boarded the bus for Tuscaloosa, Alabama, I could not help but to grasp the meaning of my journey. I was the seventh and youngest child in my family, as well as the only member of the family who would go to college. I thought about the friendly people of Marion, both Black and White. My departure from the mountains also caused me to think of my childhood and school friends: Gene Beam, Carl and Guy Jackson, Asa Owens, James and Wilma Tate, Della Johnson, Pearl Cannon, James Lindsey, Ella Sue Fowler-Young, Billy Martin, Fanny Carson, Evelyn Carson and Rosemary Avery.

I could also feel the spirit of my favorite school teacher, Ms. Bessie Greenlee. Many times Ms.Greenlee would say to her students, "Bad habits can be broken." I imagined and surmised what her encouraging words to me might be: **The bad habit of not applying yourself for success can be broken if you are willing to try.**

While riding the bus to Tuscaloosa, I remember having the audacity to think, "One way or another I am definitely going to make an impression on my fellow school mates." I felt it was inevitable because of where I was from and how I looked as a young man. Two questions came to mind. The first question was, "To what extent will I shock teachers and fellow students when they learn of my limited educational skills." The second question was, "To what degree will I dazzle the ladies with my good looks."

My arrival at Stillman and the check in at the Men's Dormitory, John Knox Hall went very smooth. The first item on the agenda was a reception for freshmen students at Geneva Hall. As I walked to the reception, I wondered if the students I'd meet would feel as I did which was apprehensive and somewhat fearful of what would lie ahead. The first person I met at the reception was Bettye Windham from Reform, Alabama. Our friendly conversation seemed to take away the jitters that had built up inside of my stomach.

While going through the reception line, the Registrar, Evelyn Nalls said to me, "Mr. Ashe, we are happy that you chose to come to Stillman for more reasons than one. We are expecting outstanding things from you." Her comments to me were surprising. Did her comments to me come about because of a conversation she had with my friend, Isaac Crosby? I did not know but I was curious. Whatever the case, Ms. Nalls' comments placed additional pressure on me to be successful at Stillman. However, the greatest motivational factor for me to succeed was because I didn't want to return to my hometown an academic failure.

Another contributing factor of my being successful at Stillman was the good fortune of having Woodrow (Max) Parker being assigned my roommate. Max and I had several things in common. For instance, he and I were from small country towns. He was from Atmore, Alabama. On the other hand, I was from a small country town located at the edge of the Blue Ridge Mountains in North Carolina. We both loved sports and held the same philosophical views on practically everything. My attempt to emulate Max's work ethics of striving for excellence allowed me to become a successful educator.

I would be remiss if I failed to mention two upper classmen who were big brothers and mentors to me during my educational journey at Stillman. They are Thomas Martin and Thurman Brown.

My Priceless Gift From Stillman College

By
Richard D. Ashe

During the course of our lives, undoubtedly, we receive gifts from our friends, family, coworkers and social affiliations. Needless to say, some of those gifts could be categorized as tangible or intangible.

At the time when recipients receive gifts, they may not fully grasp the value or magnitude of these gifts until years or decades later. Specifically and personally, I would like to reference the gift that Stillman College gave to me.

The sum total of four years of experiences that I had at Stillman College, I now see as a "priceless gift." From day one until I graduated, my Stillman experiences helped me to succeed and compete nationally in post graduate settings as well as in a highly competitive workforce.

I also thank and give credit to Stillman College for allowing me the opportunity to develop my interactive and interpersonal skills.

As it is in most educational settings, there will be pleasant and difficult challenges that confront students. How we choose to handle the challenges play a significant role in our ability to handle adversity. Reflectively, I can now say that some minor unpleasant experiences at Stillman turned out to be "blessings in disguise" because I learned valuable lessons from those experiences. Moreover, I refused to allow adversity or obstacles to get in the way of my educational goals.

It is quite obvious that obtaining a college education is an expensive undertaking. However, some experiences we receive in a college setting are priceless gifts. It would be very difficult to put a price tag on them. I submit to the premise that it is also impossible to place a dollar value on my friendships and the educational skills that I received at Stillman College. The thousands of warm and indelible impressions that I have about college life is due to my four year Stillman experience.

Thank you, Stillman College for your priceless gift and magnolia tree experiences.

Sugar Daddies On The Side

By

Annette B. Austin

Preface

The readers of the narrative below should know that the names mentioned in this story have been changed to protect the privacy of the individuals. Furthermore, this story is being shared to serve a two-fold purpose. The first of which is to generate discussions relative to dating choices and situations. The second purpose of this story is to induce discussions about the violence that's inflicted on women throughout our society.

Typically, some of the pleasant experiences that Stillman or other college students will attain are the friendships that will develop and be nourished over a long period of time. I believe this is especially true of students who choose to date for an extended period during their college experience.

My dating experience with David at Stillman was one of respect and mutual admiration for each other. We enjoyed studying together, strolling, holding hands and spending time under the giant magnolia tree that still stands in front of Sheppard Library. I was told numerous times that several girls envied me because I was dating David who was a star basketball player. He was also tall and handsome.

Several girls in my dormitory (Winsborough Hall) had boyfriends and were content to have a steady relationship with one guy. However, two roommates in Winsborough Hall, Patsy and Pearl prided themselves with having a relationship with a boy on campus as well as having "Secret Sugar Daddies" who lived off campus. It was apparent to several residents of the dormitory that the sugar daddies were more than willing to wine, dine and provide these two young ladies with the finest dress apparel on the market.

One late evening weekend, my roommate, Dorothy Hunter and I were in the snack area of the dormitory when suddenly and simultaneously the doorbell rang with a loud pounding on the front door. Upon opening the door, our dormitory mother, Ms. Evans, Dorothy and I could see the frantic look on Patsy's face. Patsy shouted for Ms. Evans to come outside quickly to the magnolia tree because Otis was threatening to beat up Pearl. Immediately, Ms. Evans dashed out the door and ran toward the magnolia tree. My roommate, Dorothy and I being the inquisitive type followed behind Ms. Evans.

When we reached the vicinity of the magnolia tree, we heard Otis say to Pearl, "You'd better tell me where you've been or I'm going up side your head." Despite the threat that Otis had made, Pearl responded very sternly. "First of all, it's none of your damn business where I've been; and secondly, you don't want to know."

At that point when Otis drew back his fist to strike Pearl, Ms. Evans with a loud and admonishing tone of voice shouted, "Stop it! Stop it! What's the problem here"? Otis responded by saying, "Ms. Evans, I love Pearl, but if she doesn't tell me where she's been tonight, I'm going to hurt her."

In a calm and soft tone of voice, Ms. Evans responded by saying, "Otis, I hear what you are saying. We can work through your words, but if you choose to strike her, you will take this situation to another level."

Ms. Evans, turned towards Dorothy and me and said, "You two go back to the dormitory." Then she said, "Pearl you go with them because I wish to speak with Otis, privately."

As we returned to the dormitory, I began to think how lucky I was to have David as a boyfriend. I also wondered about the wisdom of any girl having a steady boyfriend and a secret sugar daddy on the side.

Annette Bing Austin is a 1962 graduate of Stillman College. She obtained a Masters Degree from The College of New Jersey. (Trenton State College)

A Reality Check Under The Magnolia Tree

By
Floyd Phillips

Growing up on the south side of Tuscaloosa Alabama was special in that every family knew every other family in the community. We all looked out for each other.

There were eight of us kids plus mom and pops. By the time I grew up my oldest brother Leroy, had been in and out of the military and started a family of his own. The other two brothers had left home for college and military. My three older sisters were away at college, career or marriage leaving only myself and my youngest sister Evelyn at home.

I was a junior at Druid High School, where I played trumpet in the band like my older brother Carl had before me.

One of our immediate neighbors was Evelyn Johnson, a very kind young lady who taught math and music in a neighboring county. She would spend time with me if I had a difficult music score to learn. She was so easy going that I often felt people took advantage of her kindness.

It was in the fall of 1958 that she asked me to come over to her home to discuss a problem she was having with a boyfriend, a Stillman student who resided in John Know Hall.

When I arrived she was sitting alone in the dark. She told me that she suspected her boyfriend was involved with another young lady on campus, although he insisted that it was all her imagination. After sharing a drink with her, she convinced me to drive her to the Stillman campus. She offered me $5.00 to "jack up" this boyfriend whom I had never seen before. The deal was to confront him under the magnolia tree, if we found him with another young lady as she had suspected. You see, I considered myself to be an "ok" physical specimen at that time (6 feet and 140 pounds) and felt that could take care of me. After all, how big could he be?

We hid behind the magnolia tree about half an hour. Finally he showed up arm in arm with a young lady. Evelyn pointed him out to me. My jaws dropped. I had spent a lot of time on campus, and most of the guys I saw were about my size, but this guy had to be twice my size. At 6'1 and 250 pounds of pure muscle, he was as wide as a door way. He looked like he ate nails for breakfast and bricks for lunch. I had never seen a man this big (or so it seemed). I took another look at him and looked at my neighbor, then gave her a $5.00 refund.

Several weeks later, after getting to know him we became great friends.

Floyd Phillips received a Bachelor's Degree from Stillman College in 1964.

Extreme Revenge Under
the Magnolia Tree

By
Richard D. Ashe

Terry, a Stillman College junior commuted from his nearby home town of Alberta City to attend classes. He was what some would call "a handsome guy who was level headed and smart." On the weekends, Terry and his girl friend, Olivia, (Not their real names) who was also a junior were often seen studying and spending time together. The couple had been dating since their freshman year at Stillman. In fact the two were voted by the student body as the "Cutest Couple." Each of them was also on the Dean's List.

During a fall evening after sunset, fraternity brothers, Max Parker, Floice McKnight, Mack Salter, Henry Houze and I were in the lobby of John Knox Hall discussing the national rankings of college football teams. Suddenly, coming through the front door limping with anguish on his face was none other than the "charming," Terry. He was in obvious pain with facial scratches on his forehead.

We asked what had happened to him. His response was, "Some crabby boys attacked me for no reason at all." McKnight said, "We need to call the security guard or the police." Very quickly, Terry said, "That's okay, I'll be alright. I need to sit down for a while." Max and I invited him to come to our room until he felt better.

After putting some rubbing alcohol and Vaseline cream on his bruises and scratches, Terry said, "I'm going to level with you guys, but promise me you won't say anything about this." We all agreed that we would remain silent if this was his wish.

Somewhat hesitant, Terry began to speak. "You all know that Olivia and I have been going steady for a couple of years. Earlier today I talked this fine freshman chick, Pearl into taking a cruise with me around Lake Tuscaloosa. When we got back, I parked my car across the street and the two of us strolled to the Magnolia Tree. In less than two minutes later, I saw Olivia and her roommate, Ethel walking across the street coming back from the store with shopping bags. I quickly turned my back, hoping that she wouldn't recognize me.

In less than a minute, Olivia and her roommate, Ethel were standing in front of Pearl and me. Olivia was furious and screamed at me, "What the hell is going on under this tree?" I responded by saying, "Nothing is going on. We were just talking." Olivia then says to Pearl, "Miss bowlegged witch, I've seen you strutting around campus like you are Miss Universe. Now, you are trying to steal my man."

Pearl responded indignantly to Olivia by saying, "Wait just a minute, you dried up freckled faced frog, I don't have to steal nothing from nobody. If you don't have what it takes to keep your man, then that's your problem."

At that point Olivia and Pearl raised their fists to attack each other. I quickly stepped between the two of them and shouted, "Stop it! This is ridiculous"! Before I knew anything else, Olivia, Ethel, and Pearl began a vicious attack on me. They called me a two-timing liar, jackass, and other names I've never heard before.

The three of them began to scratch my face and kick my legs until I fell to the ground. While on the ground they kicked me in my side and stomach. These good looking ladies were acting like wild animals. Finally, I was able to pull myself off of the ground and ran as fast as I could. That's why I ran for cover at John Knox Hall. I've never seen or experienced anything like it."

After telling us about his ordeal, he reminded us of our promise to keep the incident to ourselves. Again, we assured him that his ordeal was safe with us. We agreed to walk with him to his parked car. When we got to his car it was quite obvious that those ladies had added another insult to his injuries. Two windows of his car had been broken by two huge rocks.

Terry said, "This is too much, I'm never going to speak to those girls again." On our way back to the dormitory, I said to the guys, "It is said that inside of every dark cloud there's a silver lining. I wonder where the silver lining in this situation is. Henry responded by saying, "Before the day ended, Terry had two girlfriends. Now he has none."

I said, "Well, it's better to have loved and lost, than never to have loved at all." The five of us had a hearty laugh.

<u>Postscript</u>

Needless to say, the actions of the students in this story are not typical or characteristic of the usual self assured and refined Stillmanites.

MEMORIES FOR THE AGES

"Good ideas and intentions become just that
if they aren't followed with action."

R. D. Ashe

CHAPTER THREE

Memories For The Ages

Stillman Magazine Features Three Alumni

The author of this book was quite familiar with the contributions of Stillmanites, Dr. Lena Prewitt and Lt.General Willie Williams and had spoken to them about contributing to **"Under The Magnolia Tree"** book project. I had not had the privilege of meeting Patricia Wilson. After reviewing the three features in the "Spring, 2013 Stillman Magazine," I felt compelled to get permission to include the stories of the three Stillman alumni to be included in **"Under The Magnolia Tree."**

Excerpts from the "Stillman Magazine" featuring Wilson, Williams and Prewitt are as follows:

"From Detours to Destiny - Patricia Wilson Shows the Way
By
Mary Sood

In 11th grade, Patricia Wilson wrote down everything she planned to accomplish in life. She intended to go to college, graduate, get married and have two children, and forge a riveting career in business. Eventually Wilson reached or exceeded all of her goals. She has been happily married for 19 years, and has a job that she loves. But on her way to a wonderful life, she occasionally veered off course. And like a player in Milton Bradley's Game of Life, she found herself temporarily holding the wrong career cards.

Cosmetology school, for example, was "just something I thought I would do," she says with a dismissive wave of her well-manicured hands. A stint in housekeeping was a more logical detour. Her oldest son had childhood asthma, and was often ill. Although he was covered by his father's insurance, she felt it was important to have additional coverage so she joined the housekeeping staff at DCH Regional Medical Center. That was three college degrees and nearly two decades ago.

In 1996, Wilson came to Stillman as a secretary, which placed her squarely on the career path she envisioned for herself years earlier and allowed her to quickly reach both her academic and professional goals.

"I worked full-time at Stillman College. I had a 6 year old and an 8 month old, and I went to Shelton State Community at night; had a course at Stillman during work hours; and took classes in SMI (Stillman Management Institute) on Tuesday evenings," says Wilson.

She applauds SMI for meeting the educational needs of adult learners with transferable credits who are often employed full or part-time and desire to complete their degrees in the evening.

"SMI faculty really motivated and inspired me. If students needed tutoring, they put in extra hours to help us. We were successful as a result of their commitment to us," says Wilson ho was also encouraged by Dr. Charlotte Carter (Dean of Arts and Sciences at the time) and others who knew that she was a first generation college student. "I was enrolled in three programs at the same time. I finished Stillman in three years, while working full-time, and graduated Magna Cum laude. I was married with two kids when I started, and I had three by the time I graduated. My husband and I built our home by the time our youngest was one. I was young, aggressive and ambitious because I wanted more for my family."

Wilson now serves as Stillman's Human Resources Director and as an adjunct professor for Southern New Hampshire University and for the Stillman Management Institute. (SMI). Today, as she sits confidently in her office in Batchelor Building, skillfully managing every aspect of Human Resources, it is difficult to envision her scouring sinks at the hospital.

But getting from where she was to where she is required and intense recommitment to achieving her goals. Before she could frame her B.A. in Business Administration, Wilson enrolled in an on-line graduate program at Troy University. Shortly before finishing her Master of Public Administration in 2003, she was promoted to her position in Human Resources. She promptly began working on another degree at Troy University—a Master of Science in Human Resource Management, which she completed in 2008. She will quadruple her goal of earning a college degree when she finishes her Doctorate of Business Administration at Walden University in a few years. Wilson's commitment to her plan has never precluded taking on additional challenges. When she was asked to oversee Stillman's dance team in 2000, and the cheerleaders in 2004, she accepted both offers. "I never cheered, never danced and never twirled, but I'm good at multitasking and I have good organizational skills," says Wilson. She downplays her amazing versatility and laudable commitments to the College by adding, "One day I saw Dr. McNealey on campus in jeans, cutting shrubs. The president's dedication inspired me."

Although her advancement from housekeeping to Human Resources sounds almost like a fairy tale, Wilson knows that preparation trumps wishful thinking. She believes in having a vision, writing it down, and understanding that the bumps you encounter en route to your destiny will give you a testimony to share with those who may be a few steps behind you on a similar road. Wilson states, " No matter how old or young you are, there is an opportunity to have a different outcome in your life. Map out a plan and see what you need to accomplish to get to where you want to be. It will take commitment, dedication and sacrifice. But the only way you can receive what God has for you is to be prepared."

Patricia Wilson is living proof that no matter how many detours you may have taken, it is never too late to reach your chosen destination.

In Pursuit of Excellence
By
Lt. General Willie Williams

At a certain stage in life, people must choose an activity or career with particular meaning to them, and most importantly, to their community or greater society; otherwise they will live a less fulfilled life because it will be built on a narrow perspective. Dr. King once said, "When you discover what you will be in your life, set out to do it as if God Almighty called you at that particular moment in history to do it." So, we shouldn't set out to do a good job but rather set out to do the very best job within the capabilities and capacity we have been given.

I can assure you it was not a smooth ride for me to get to where I serve today. There were many bumps along the way. As a young boy from Moundville, Alabama, I never envisioned that I would be able to attend college and achieve the rank of Lieutenant General in the United States Marine Corps. I am one of only two African Americans currently serving, and one of four ever to wear that rant in the history of the Marine Corps. By not quitting doing my best, and seeking the help of mentors when in difficulty, I found that excellence was within reach. And I learned attributes that can be attained and practiced by all.

FOCUSED VISION

In figuring out your path, you should look inside of your very being, and see "greatness" and "excellence." Not necessarily what you see in others, but what you see as possible within yourself because each person's path to excellence is different. However, I do believe there is a common formula to excellence. Despite one's path, there must be a vision and there must be preparation. Throughout life, opportunities will show themselves. But they will be wasted if you are not prepared to take advantage of them, and have the inner strength of conviction and determination to drive to excellence within those opportunities.

EXCELLENCE

Excellence is tied to the choices we make through our life's journey, driven by our vision and perseverance. Nothing worthwhile is easy, so I caution that no one of achievement has avoided failures and disappointments. But we keep at it, learn from mistakes, and never quit.

FOCUS

Whether it's starting a business, running a business, fixing people, things, or situations, running for office or raising a family, remember that making your mark on and in the world is not easy. It takes special patience and commitment, and an understanding that success comes with plenty of setbacks and failures. Focus is one of the keys. Given that life is full of challenges, we must be able to control distractions.

There will be times when unexpected voices will try to convince you that you can't make a difference; that your sights are too high considering your background and socioeconomic status. Don't buy it! Stay the course, and know that you are better than that. Look deep inside and know that you are more than capable.

PREPARATION

With all the obstacles to be faced, preparation and deep self-examination will help with goal setting and ensure that you are well equipped to conquer all the distractions life brings your way. Don't be afraid to seek guidance and mentorship from different people, in different industries and backgrounds to gain a well rounded perspective on life. By reaching out to different folks from different walks of life, you expand your horizon, eventually allowing new vistas (while improving your contact base). However, that expansion brings risk and temptations, which must also be managed. But never compromise your own moral principles or the moral authority of your institution, your employer, or the Nation.

LOYALTY

Yes, I said "Nation." Regardless of your profession, you're always (as long as you are a citizen of this country) a representative of this great Nation. Opportunities to compromise your principles will be plentiful as will opportunities to do the easy thing or the popular thing, especially when no one is looking. Every day we witness headlines filled with individuals and organizations who failed their own test - folk who failed to demonstrate personal courage or failed to do what is morally and legally sound. Don't let such distractions derail "your pursuit of happiness;" rather, keep things in perspective. What is important in life is life itself. Enjoy life, do the things you enjoy the most whenever you can.

PREPARATION & EDUCATION

However, always remember preparation is a continuous circle. Opportunities in life will present themselves and those prepared will be the ones taking advantage of them. So preparation includes education, since "education is the key." However, education not only in the classroom setting, but lifelong education in the broader sense as well. Talk to experts, read the news, and ask questions not only of those who decide the issues, but of everyday people as well.

COMMITMENT

Throughout our pursuit of excellence, we must continuously evaluate and reevaluate our short and long-term goals, and remain committed to achieving them, because life will not always go as planned. Remain flexible and committed to your end goals and persistent in execution. Be receptive to change.

When I joined the Marine Corps, and after deciding to make it a career, my goal was to be a Major in 20 years. At the time, that is what I thought was achievable. But as I grew, I realized that I could not only reach that goal, I could go further as long as I continued preparing and applying myself. And now I find myself five promotions and 19 years beyond my initial goal.

Once you have achieved excellence in your endeavor, you must manage it and take care of your responsibilities and yourself—spiritually, physically, and emotionally. The more responsibilities you have, the more hectic life can become. So be careful to maintain a balance; value family and friends, as they are your most dependable support when things get complicated. Give back to your institution, family, community and country. Keep that "team spirit" attitude for life, and help others in pursuit of their excellence with the same opportunities you have and will have.

The Extraordinary Life and Times of Dr. Lena Prewitt
By
Mary Sood

In a crowded room, people tend to gravitate toward Dr. Lena Prewitt. She claims to be an ordinary person, but no one believes her. For the past five decades, this former Stillman student, professor and administrator has been a prominent speaker on manufacturing, education, equal rights and international relations. She has visited 60 countries, lectured in South Korea, Jordan and Egypt; and participated in advisory state commissions to China, India, South Africa and Poland. At 82, she has a gentle face that belies the stubborn spirit that propelled her to achieve what should have been unachievable for an African American woman born in Wilcox County, Alabama in the 1930s.

Someone once playfully proclaimed that if you rest your palm on Dr. Prewitt's hand, her wisdom will be passed on to you. Although touching her hand probably won't help you, her former students do claim that being in her classroom transformed their lives. Stillman alumni Betty Brown Williamson and her husband, the late Coy Williamson, were both profoundly influenced by Dr. Prewitt. "She told us we could do anything, and we took her at her word. In 1974 we opened an 8-bay car wash. We bought another building in 1982 and opened a 120-bed nursing home in Atlanta. In 2000, we built a brand new funeral home. In 2002, we bought a second funeral home in Riverdale, Georgia. All of this happened because she made us believe we could be anything we wanted to be."

Although Williamson recognized immediately that Dr. Prewitt was an excellent professor, some students needed time to reflect upon and reevaluate the impact she had on their lives. "Once, when I was on a plane, a man tapped me on the shoulder and said, "I am one of your former students," Dr. Prewitt recalls. He went on to say, "I hated you when I was in your class. When I graduated, I hated you. Now I want you to know that you were the best teacher I ever had. Your making me learn problem solving by case analysis took me straight to the top of my career."

The success Dr. Prewitt inspired in her students is perhaps a direct reflection of her own tenacity and determination to combat seemingly insurmountable obstacles. "As a child, I automatically, instinctively rebelled against people saying what I couldn't do because I was a female or because I was a minority. In those days, females had little input into decision-making. We were bound by rules made by men. We were expected to stay home and wash, clean and cook. I liked to hunt, walk in the woods and swim. I liked reading, but we had little to read other than the newspaper."

Although her father encouraged her to act "like a girl" he also motivated her to be a leader. "My parents were poor and had nothing, but they gave us good values," she says.

In high school, after studying Henry David Thoreau's thoughts on a successful work life, she said she wanted to be like Thoreau. Her father replied, "If you learn to do a job better than any one else, you will always have a job. But the person who knows why the job is being done will be your boss. You strive to be the boss."

'My most important focus is thinking. At Stillman, there were good teachers such as Dr. (Albert) Winn and Dr. (Samuel) Franklin who taught me how to think, study and learn. Dean Hardy and his wife civilized me. Dr. (Martha) Vardeman gently corrected my English. For example, I would say, "I coulda came" and she would smile and say, "I could have come." So I grasped the understanding that one has to speak properly."

In her senior year, when she told President Samuel Burney Hay she planned to graduate, find employment and provide financial assistance to her family, he laughed and said she was going to graduate school. The idea did not sound feasible. She had no money, universities in the South did not accept African American students, and few Black universities had graduate programs. Fortunately, after she graduated in 1954, Dr. Hay secured money for her, and she headed to Indiana University. She earned a Master's Degree in business education in 1955, the year Rosa Parks refused to sit in the back of a bus, and a doctoral degree in 1961, three years before the Civil Rights Act declared segregation illegal.

Dr. Prewitt, became a professor at Stillman at 26, and later became the first African American female faculty member at the University of Alabama. Eventually, she returned to Stillman as Chair of the Department of Business and Economics and as Vice President of Financial Affairs.

She says, "There are only two things that are really important - developing yourself and contributing to the lives of others. I have met with people all over the world. I am comfortable with all cultures and I respect all people. It is fascinating to see how much we are all alike and how much we are different. I wonder and reflect on what we have to do to have more unity in diversity."

Stillman's First Encounter with the Civil Rights Issue

By
Richard D. Ashe

During the early 60's African American College students across the nation were staging protest marches against the laws of segregation. Although the students at Stillman had not participated in any protest of significance, nevertheless, they were quite knowledgeable of what was happening nationally. The national television news programs and the local "Tuscaloosa News" were quite popular.

Stillman students were able to see and read about college students engaging in marches, sit in's and boycotts. A few students felt the need to become involved but there was no organized effort to do so. After all, they had been warned by the way of a telephone call to the men's dormitory that if Stillman students came downtown to protest, the Klu Klux Klan would be waiting. Students knew that Tuscaloosa was the home and headquarters of the "fearful," Imperial Wizard of the Klan.

An impromptu decision on the part of three female students brought Stillman into the Civil Rights era. At the corner of 36th Street and directly across from Snedicar Hall was a bus stop that many students utilized to drop them off and pick them up after classes. Upon getting on the bus, instead of going to the back as usual, they decided to sit up front. The bus driver requested that they move to the back, they ignored him. The driver's decision was to remain parked at that location rather than drive with the students sitting up front.

Information about the situation at the bus stop spread rather quickly. Students rushed to the scene and began cheering and chanting their support for what was happening. After an hour or so, several police officers arrived at the scene and directed the students to leave the bus. The students complied with the officer's request. To a large extent, the decision of those three students caused a sigh of relief for many. No longer would they have to say that Stillman students had done nothing to foster the efforts of the civil rights movement.

Two days later an announcement was made for students to report to Birthright Auditorium for an important meeting. At that meeting, and as usual the assembly program began with a reading from the Scriptures, prayer and announcements.

Dr. Samuel B. Hay, the president of Stillman College then took charge of the meeting and spoke to the student body. In a somber and apologetic tone of voice, he said that he understood the efforts of the civil rights movement. However, his job as President was to be able to raise funds and maintain funding sources for the college.

Dr. Hay indicated that rather than lose major financial support for the college, he had no choice but to forbid Stillman students from participating in any further demonstrations. After Dr. Hay made those comments there were murmuring sounds all over the auditorium. A student requested the opportunity to speak. His response was, "Dr. Hay, I am disappointed in the position that you have taken."

"If this is the position that the donors are taking in the Civil Rights struggle, then they should keep their money." The student received a thunderous applause and was followed by other students citing similar views.

In view of the passionate statements of students, I found myself torn at what I was seeing. Students were literally berating our president. Dr. Hay was my hero who had come to my financial rescue during an unexpected financial crises. I admired Dr. Hay for the way he stood on stage and listened to the verbal and passionate viewpoints of students without the slightest hint of being offended at what they were saying to him.

I realized the type of position that Dr. Hay found himself. He was "caught between a rock and a hard spot." He felt the need to maintain the financial stability of the college. On the other hand, students wanted him on their side to help eliminate discrimination. I had the greatest respect and admiration for Dr. Hay, but I also wanted segregation laws to end.

I will always consider Dr. Hay to have been an outstanding leader and a man of integrity. He touched the lives of thousands of students in a positive way.

My Stillman Memories

By

James Toombs

Making the Grade was Difficult at Times

The professor of Anatomy and Physiology was very stern and strict. His exams and assignments were very comprehensive.

This particular athlete had received a failing grade. (Let us call his name John). John needed to pass this class to remain eligible to participate in extra curricular activities. John made an appointment to talk with the professor concerning his grade. He wanted to know just what he could do to get a passing grade. The professor gave him a very extensive (lengthy) and comprehensive assignment which included researching the functions of the nerves and muscles of the human body.

John completed the fifteen (15) page assignment and gave it to the professor. The professor scanned the pages and said: It looks good.

I will do a more detailed check and let you know how it will affect your final grade.

The following Saturday afternoon was a very beautiful and sunny spring day. Most of the students were lingering and lounging around on the campus as usual. The professor came walking down the sidewalk outside the campus. He spotted (noticed) John a distance away on campus. He yelled with a loud voice across the campus to John. "John I got a brand new grade for you." John yells back, "You do?" The professor yells back, "Yes, John! Congratulations!! "You got a D-"

All the students on campus eyes became fixed on John. Some said what kind of grade is that to let everyone know. It must be difficult to earn a passing grade in his class.

Unforgivable or Unforgettable

I was enrolled in an archery class. You know the class where you learn to shoot the bow and arrow. After completing the theory portion of the class, it came time to learn how to actually shoot and hit the target. One day the class was practicing how to shoot the bow, cows were grazing in a pasture beyond the archery targets. (Let's call this student Tom). Tom missed the target soooo bad he hit a cow grazing in the pasture beyond the targets. Imagine that.

Later Tom learned to shoot archery accurately. He could even hit the center of the Target - the bulls eye. He still failed the class probably because of the cow incident. He repeated the class and made an A. The cows had been moved to another location.

Richard D. Ashe, Ph.D

Game Changer or Grade Changer

I was enrolled in an English Composition class and was struggling. An elderly lady was the professor. Each class meeting following an assignment to write a composition concerning a certain topic, the professor selected the most notable or outstanding paper and that student read it during the class. Points were given to students who made positive or constructive responses to questions asked. It was almost mid-semester and my composition had not been chosen once to read and I had not done well responding to questions. The professor gave an assignment to write a composition using your imagination. I chose to write about myself. I was a fugitive without a stable home.

I noticed when I walked into the classroom two weeks after the assignment; the professor fixed her eyes on me until I reached my seat and intermittently would stare at me. I began to become very concerned as to what was going on. When time came to recognize the most outstanding composition she called my name. Mr.Toombs, would you please come and read your composition? Midway through reading my composition, I glanced at the professor. She had tears settling in her eyes. After I concluded reading the composition the professor asked me with a trembling voice and eyes streaming with tears; Mr. Toombs are you really a fugitive? I responded, no ma'm. She said, I'm so glad you're not!! Now class, that is what I call really using your imagination. For the remainder of the semester I was the E. F. Hutton of the class. The professor gave me special attention when I responded to questions. My final grade was a B+

Sunday Afternoon Showdown

It was a beautiful sunny Sunday afternoon and most of the students were hanging out on campus. A young man had come to visit his high school girlfriend which was attending Stillman College. They were sitting underneath a beautiful magnolia tree. Every student at Stillman knew that the young lady had met and was dating a young man at Stillman. So, the whole campus anxiously waiting to see just what was going to happen when the Stillman man came on the scene. I mean it was like a "High Noon Showdown." Girls were all watching from the girls' dormitory windows. All eyes were fixed on the couple underneath the magnolia tree.

The Stillman man came and noticed the couple under the magnolia tree. He looked closer and saw that it was supposedly his girlfriend sitting with another young man. He walked slowly over to the couple. He greeted the young man politely. Then he extended his hand out confidently to the young lady. She grabbed his hand and pulled herself up to him. They locked arms and walked away. The campus went wild with cheers and applauses.

James Toombs received a Bachelor of Arts Dgreee from Stillman College and a Masters of Science in Administration and Supervision from Nova University.

Dean Of Students on the Prowl for Chapel Violators

By
Frederick Blackburn

One reason that my parents were delighted that I agreed to accept an athletic scholarship at Stillman College was the strict religious values that the college maintained. It was a known fact that all students knew of the chapel attendance policy. Each student also knew the consequences of violating this policy.

In fact, some students felt that it was easier to be forgiven for some major school infractions than it was for violating the Chapel Attendance Policy. At orientation, students were informed that not attending chapel for a set number of sessions during a semester could be grounds for suspension or expulsion. It didn't matter whether you were an honor student or a student who held an athletic scholarship.

Ms. Louise Mckinney, the Dean of Students was in charge of enforcing the chapel regulations; and students knew of her reputation of being intolerant of students who failed to fulfill chapel attendance requirements. The Tiger's Den located directly across the street from the campus was a popular place for students to socialize, study or listen to popular music played on the juke box. It was also a place for students to get a quick snack or purchase a variety of personal items.

One morning during the scheduled time of chapel, I decided to go to The Tiger's Den and hang out with some friends. After settling in to participate in the latest gossip or sports stories, a student who was looking out the window, shouted, "Here comes Ms. Mckinney." We all got up and saw Ms. McKinney standing at the edge of the street waiting for cars to pass before crossing the street. In a split second all of the students except for me, dashed out the front door and ran down the street before Ms. McKinney could safely cross the street.

Their swift exit from the Tiger's Den was certainly comparable to individuals responding to an emergency situation. The other students decided to run rather than put themselves in jeopardy of disciplinary action. However, I decided to stay and give Ms. Mckinney a reason for not being in chapel. As she entered the door, she looked surprised at my calm demeanor.

After staring at me with a probing look, she said to me, "Young man, what is your name and why aren't you at chapel service?" In a cool and confident tone of voice, I said, "I didn't attend school today." At that point, the look of disgust and agitation showed on her face.

After Ms. McKinney gave me a five minute lecture on the importance of attending classes and taking advantage of a college education, she left by saying to me, "Mr. Blackburn, I trust that from now on you will see fit to do the right thing; and I intend to keep abreast of the progress that you are making at Stillman."

After my Tiger's Paw experience with Ms. McKinney, I made sure that I not only met the chapel attendance requirements but the class attendance regulations as well. To have done less, I certainly would have found myself receiving another stern lecture from the Dean of Students and possibly disciplinary action.

Over the years since my encounter with Ms. Mckinney, I came to appreciate the diligence with which she performed the duties of her position. She reinforced the teachings of my parents, which were: "Be true to your goals, values and family expectations."

Ms. Mckinney's lecture also instilled in me to prepare myself in order to take advantage of opportunities when they arise.

Frederick Blackburn, a 1963 graduate of Stillman College is pastor of Holly Spring Missionary Baptist Church, Tuscaloosa, Alabama.

Remember When.....

By
Doris Hunter Metcalf

Remember When ...

Of all of the memories that I have made during my lifetime, those that were made during my Freshman and Junior years at Stillman are some of my most memorable treasures.

Since those cherished years, I have returned and relived many of those memories.

Come now, and return with me to those years of 1958 -1962.

Remember when ...

You were a Freshman "Crab" who was obligated to respond to every whim of the upperclassmen including trying to blow out the cafeteria lights.

Richard D. Ashe, Ph.D

Remember when …

John Knox for men and Winsborough and Geneva Halls for women were the only dormitories on campus.

Remember when …

You had 3 roommates all of whom had different sleep time, different wake time, different study time and different bath times.

Remember when …

You stayed up 'til the wee hours in the morning studying for Mrs. Chermock's biology test and how your roommate protested when you took that formaldehyde cat to the room to prepare for your Comparative Anatomy practical.

Remember when …

Dating in Winsborough Hall was an open room where 5 or 6 couples spent the better part of their Sunday evening, gazing into each other's eyes and sneaking a kiss or two or three.

Remember when ...

A nightly trip from the canteen always included a romantic stop beneath the Magnolia trees in front of Sheppard Library.

Remember when ...

You kept the 10 O'clock dormitory curfew rules to avoid facing the wrath of Mrs. Louise McKinney.

Remember when ...

You borrowed a penny from five people in the dorm and exchanged them for a nickel to buy a Coke.

Remember when ...

You "slow dragged" to Brook Benton's "The Same One" and "So Close" and Jerry Butler's "Your Precious Love" and be-bopped to Bobby Day's "Rockin Robin" and Lonely Teardrops" by Jackie Wilson.

Remember when ...

As a junior when you checked the freshman "Crabs" out for a possible new serious relationship and how you dumped your old love back home.

Remember when ...

You were required to sign out to go to the canteen, sign in when you returned and sign out to record your required attendance at Brown Memorial Presbyterian Church.

Remember when ...

These years ended and you were left with the task of putting everything in perspective to begin your senior year and your preparation for the Big, Brave New World called Life.

Remember "Our memories are the paradise from which we can never be expelled"

Jean Paul Richter—novelist and humorist.

Doris Hunter Metcalf, a 1962 graduate of Stillman College received a Masters degree from Ohio State University and the Ed.S degree from the University of North Alabama.

Campus Security Back in the Day

By
Richard D. Ashe

During the early 1960's the night security responsibility would usually lie on the shoulders of the security guard, Willshoot. (Not his real name) Willshoot's nickname was given to him by students due to the use of his shotgun during an incident that took place on campus several years earlier.

Willshoot's night security attire is probably noteworthy to alumni who didn't get the opportunity to actually see him. His work apparel and appearance was the image of a western movie cowboy. He wore his western style hat on the side of his head. His long handle pistol rested on the right side of his body inside of a gun holster. His footwear consisted of large leather zigzag cowboy boots. Over his left shoulder was a punch clock that was housed inside of a leather casing. In his left hand he always carried a shot gun.

On one side of Willshoot's jaw was always packed with chewing tobacco. When he spoke, his mouth was twisted to one side to hold the tobacco in the other jaw. Part of his duties as security was to assist the women's dormitory mothers at Winsborough and Geneva Hall after on campus evening activities. At the conclusion of an activity at Birthright Auditorium, the ladies were required to be inside of their dormitory within fifteen minutes.

At the conclusion of an evening activity, many ladies were escorted to their dormitory by smiling young men. The front porch at Winsborough Hall was always full with couples getting that last minute kiss and embrace. The dormitory mother's signal for the ladies to come inside was to open the door. If the dorm mother was late opening the door, Willshoot would yell very loud and sternly, **"Ya'll git on inside, right now!"** Needless to say, the couples released their embrace and the ladies went immediately inside. After this ritual took place at Winsborough Hall, Willshoot walked slowly and purposely to Geneva Hall to give the same command and get the same results. The students had heard of Willshoot's impatient temperament and didn't dare challenge his authority.

Student Boycott and Shutdown of Stillman (1969)

By

Richard D. Ashe

During the late 1960s the country's educational institutions of higher education witnessed and experienced a student movement never seen in the country's history. To give the reader a general idea of the student movement and climate of the issues during that period of time, the author of this book has chosen to give a brief synopsis of student protest that took place at two major universities, Columbia University, located in New York City and Duke University located in Durham, North Carolina. Hopefully, this will give the reader a better understanding of the issues that also led to the student boycott and shutdown of Stillman College in 1969.

Columbia University Protests of 1968

The Columbia University Protests of 1968 were among many student demonstrations that occurred around the world in that year. The Columbia protests erupted over the spring of that year after students discovered links between the university and institutional apparatus supporting the United States' involvement in the Vietnam War. The protests resulted in the student occupation of several university buildings.

Duke University Protests of 1969

The 1969 take over of the Allen Building, Duke University's administrative center, came at a time of high tension on college campuses across the nation. African-American and White students demanded a greater voice on issues ranging from course offerings to residential life.

Stillman College Protests of 1969

Although Stillman was a small, private, Presbyterian supported college, it was not immune from issues and protests that students and administrators faced at other institutions. Although this writer was a faculty member at the time of the protests, efforts were made to get several Stillman alumni from that period of time to give their input for this story. However, attempts to get a commitment to do so failed. The opinion of this writer is that although the Stillman protests took place decades ago, memories for some were still too painful to go on record to express their views.

The student protests was one of the most media covered stories about Stillman. This writer visited Stillman's archives to examine the College's official version of the protests. Below is a condensed version of the student protests that appears in the archives at Stillman. The names of students, faculty and staff members who were major subjects of the protests have been intentionally omitted by this author to protect their privacy.

Chronology of Events

February 17,--- President Harold Stinson received a letter accompanied by a petition at 12: noon that demanded a reply in writing by 3:00 p.m. with a verbal ultimatum that if the demands weren't met, the students would boycott classes and the cafeteria. Dr. Stinson got the demands when he was leaving the office for a meeting with the college architect in Birmingham.

February 19, --- Upon Dr. Stinson's return, a meeting was arranged between student leaders and the administration. A second list of grievances was presented which students said was to clarify the first list.

The meeting lasted more than four hours. The complaints included were poor preparation and lack of variety in cafeteria food, against food service; that specific individuals of the administration, the postmistress and business office were not showing the proper courtesy to which students were entitled.

February 20, --- Students attempted to present a new petition calling for all Student Government Association officers be declared "Null and Void." Dr. Stinson indicated that if students wished to vacate offices they would have to do it within the frame work of the constitution and bylaws. Issues raised in the new petition included: Sufficient and competent faculty and administration members; investigation of financial aid and business departments; complaints of living conditions in dormitories. Dr. Stinson agreed to present answers in writing no later than February 22.

February 21, --- Students implemented a boycott that included the college cafeteria. It was about this time that intimidation and harassment of students not participating in the boycott. Students bombarded the news media with releases and telephone calls. In many cases the list given to the media were different from lists given to Dr. Stinson. Boycotting students called on merchants and townspeople for money and support for the boycott.

February 21, --- Students staged a sit-in on the gym floor, forcing a cancellation of the Stillman-Dillard basketball game. Then they moved to the college center where a sleep –in was staged. Appeals to the students to return to their dorms by Dr. Stinson and a local minister were ignored. Intimidation and harassment were stepped up. In some cases, students wishing to return to their dormitories were prevented. Students locked the doors from the inside with chains and locks. Guards with billy clubs patrolled the building and challenged entry to the building.

Dr. Stinson met with student leaders who refused to allow him to meet with all students. They not only rejected answers but a new list of demands calling for the firing of eight more faculty and staff members. One student then told Dr. Stinson that his time was up for the meeting that he would have to escort him from the building. The student was armed with a night stick.

February 22 --- Dr. Stinson responded to a list of demands submitted by the leader of the boycott. Some of the topics he addressed were: Food Service, Tiger's Den, Faculty-Student Ratio, and Maintenance in the residence halls: John Knox Hall, Geneva and Winsborough Halls.

February 23, --- At 9:45 a.m. the machinery for closing the school was put in effect. An announcement was made that the school was closed to students and faculty. Students were asked to vacate the premises by 6:00 p.m. Telegrams were sent to all parents informing them of the decision to close the school. More than 100 newsmen representing the major wire services and TV networks were on hand for an expected confrontation between students and police.

Two pre-fabricated buildings leased by the college were damaged by fire. The equipment in two of the buildings was destroyed valued in excess of $10,000. "The Liberator" (Student underground newspaper) praised the bravery of the individuals who carried out the destruction.

March 10, --- The school reopened with students having to meet with designated college officials; and to sign pledges to follow rules and regulations of the school. In the meantime, hearings were held for suspended students by five faculty and staff members and two students. An example of the charges brought against the students included:

1. You interrupted the normal operation of Hay Center to leave the premises at regular closing hour; you barricaded yourself in the building and refused to leave although repeatedly asked to do so.

2. You halted the operation of the post office in Hay College Center.

3. You received travel money from the college business office for the avowed purpose of leaving the campus after official closing of the college, but instead you returned to barricade yourself in Hay College Center.

Of the 732 students who returned, nine withdrew and another 26 were suspended or expelled, leaving a student body of 697 on April 3, 1969.

* Reference: Stillman College Archives

Stillman Librarian Robert Heath is Driven by Joy of Helping Others

By

Ed Enoch, Staff Writer of the Tuscaloosa News

6/29/14

Robert Heath, Stillman College's dean of libraries, is on the cusp of a 50-year career between the stacks at his alma mater with no plans to retire anytime soon.

"When I think of Stillman College, I think of Robert Heath. As for as I am concerned, he is an intellectual giant," said Richard Ashe, a retired principal from Georgia public schools and a Stillman alumnus.

Ashe is working with Heath to gather research for a collection of accounts from Stillman alumni of their time on campus. The book is titled "Under the Magnolia Tree," a reference to the trees on the green space in front of the library.

The men's time as students overlapped, and Ashe said the two have been friends for decades.

Ashe treasures his friend as an encyclopedic resource on the college's history.

Seemingly quick questions are invitations to history lessons. Heath enthusiastically rattles off details of significant characters and events in Stillman's history. Some, such as the story of the Birthrights, freed slaves turned landowners who bequeathed hundreds of acres of Missouri farmland to the college, come from the library's collections. Others, such as a student protest on campus in the late 1960s, are Heath's firsthand experiences as a staff member or student.

The 76- yearold, who has been employed as a librarian at the small private Presbyterian college since 1966, attributes his long tenure to providence.

Heath attended Atlanta University, now Clark Atlanta University, for graduate school and was working at Alabama State University in 1966 when Stillman instructor and former roommate approached him about returning to his alma mater.

"It really wasn't on my mind," Heath said, adding he was comfortably established at ASU.

But the young librarian talked it over with his wife, who was interested in graduate school at the University of Alabama. There was an appeal to returning to the campus that had endeared itself with its family environment, Heath said. The young couple only planned to return to Tuscaloosa for a few years. But once back, opportunities such as working with the Southern Association of Colleges and Schools as a library consultant kept appearing and a brief stop turned into a career for Heath.

"That's why I keep using that term, providential, because things kept happening," he said.

Heath defers the question of retirement to divine planning as well.

"I will leave it up to him. I do believe God intervenes in the lives of his children," he said.

Heath, who grew up in Anniston and Gadsden, came to the college in 1957, after spending a year working to save money for college.

Heath learned about Stillman from a teacher in Gadsden, who was the sister of the head librarian Martha O'Rourke. The librarian became one of Heath's mentors on campus, helping him toward graduate school and a career as a librarian. Until years later, Heath said he was unaware of the familial connection between his mentor and his former teacher in Gadsden.

"All of these things just lined up…it was just meant for me to be a librarian," he said.

Heath approached the prospect of college with a heady confidence.

At the time, I thought there was nothing I couldn't do. I thought I could go to any school and set the woods on fire," he said.

He wanted to work in the library and was selected as a student worker.

"When I first came here, I wanted to be an elementary school teacher," Heath said. "That all went out the window when I started working here."

In the 1960 yearbook, Heath's senior profile lists his aspiration as librarian. An aptitude test taken during his freshman year includes librarian among the list of likely careers. Heath said he finally saw the results of the test as a senior after his goal was already set.

"When I saw (the test results), I said, 'This is it,'" Heath said.

One of the early draws was being around people working on projects that seemed full of purpose.

"I just wanted to be a part of that. When they finished their paper, it's your paper too," he joked.

Heath remains proud of his ability to locate books for library visitors.

"I was able to go find anything," he said.

Heath was hooked on helping library-goers as a student worker.

"When I look in their eyes and something lights up…It was very satisfying to be of service to somebody," he said.

Sitting in his office, a cardboard file box at his elbow and a yearbook with a splitting spine before him, Heath recalled a phone call from a woman in Europe who was searching for a photo of a relative. The woman cried when the librarian was able to find a photo for her.

"I had this experience over and over and over again," he said.

Heath's love of helping people is part of a general philosophy and spiritual mandate to serve others.

"I am a religious person and that is what I think God wants us to do," he said.

The work also appeals to his affinity for the details.

"I'm a stickler for details," he said.

It's an important trait for librarians, Heath said. He related his experience in a cataloging course in graduate school. His professor kept returning his assignment, a sample catalog card, as incorrect but without an explanation. Heath would pour over his card again looking for the mistake.

"That was their method of instruction – discovery," he said.

He had added an unnecessary period behind the author's name, incorrectly signaling the writer was dead.

"It took me a week to see that period," Heath said.

The details and the system of order to keep track of a library full of information appealed to his sense of challenge.

"I take people's requests very seriously. If it was not important, they would not have asked for it," he said.

Heath noted his recent work with Ashe to track down details about former students for the book, including yearbook photos and information about the student occupation of campus buildings in 1969.

Stillman was among institutions nationwide that saw students protesting for a greater say in campus affairs, according to Ashe "I had a lot of fun looking up that boycott. It brought up some memories," Heath said.

Heath was on staff and remembered President Harold N. Stinson coming into the staff meeting to announce the college was closed. Heath also recalls a call from his father, who instructed his son to collect his sister, who was among the students who had occupied the Hay Center.

Heath believes details are important because an account will stand as a record for years to come.

"As long as it is in digital, that story will be told and we want it to be right," he said.

As he collected alumni accounts of their time as students, Ashe wanted to include Heath. Heath declined, Ashe said, suggesting he give the honor to someone else. Ashe also tried previously to give his friend a gift as a token of appreciation, but Heath recommended a donation to Stillman instead.

"It's not about him, it's about the college and the service he wants to render to the college," Ashe said. "His life I would say is God, family and Stillman."

Stillman College Will Always Remain First in My Heart

By
Robert E. Burns

I was a young man who grew up on the outskirts of the City of Tuscaloosa, what is now called "Old Greensboro Road." We lived several yards from our "Home" church, and I often recall, that following church services, and dinner at home, one of my younger aunts, a cousin and I would return to sit on the church steps. We would sit there and watch people go by in their cars on their Sunday afternoon drives. As we sat there watching, I'd always say, "One day I'm going to have a nice car to take my family on Sunday afternoon drives." This motivation, along with that of my family, is what inspired me to want to do well and excel in my studies so that I could go to college, for even then, I knew that college was the stepping stone to a better life.

Even though several of my family members had attended and finished from Stillman, I applied to Tuskegee in order to participate in their Air Force ROTC program, and was accepted. However, our home burned the year before I was to enter, and this made it impossible for my parents to pay Tuskegee's tuition. Stillman was in my future.

Shortly after I entered Stillman in the fall of September 1960, I knew I was in the right place. The first two years as a commuting and working student were somewhat of a challenge. Unlike most students today who have cars, I and most of my beloved Stillmanites were carless, so transportation to and from school was often an issue.

After completing my first two years at Stillman, finance became an issue. I joined the Air Force and completed a four year tour, but there was never any doubt that I would return to Stillman and complete my college education, which I did in 1968.

Stillman laid the solid foundation that enabled me to move on, to move up, and to do better enabling me to achieve the things I have. I will forever be grateful to instructors like Dr. Jaspeth Hall, who pushed us to excel in mathematics, Dr. William Venable, an excellent physics professor, Mrs. Ottilie C. Chermock, who pushed us to the extreme in biology, and Mrs. Elizabeth Etchison, who gave us a better understanding of the Book of Luke and Christian Ethics.

Even though Stillman was not my first choice, it will always remain first in my heart. Thank you Stillman and may God continue to bless You!!

Robert E. Burns received the Bachelor of Science Degree from Stillman College in 1968.

MAGNOLIA PRESSURE
AND INFLUENCE

"Wise is the person who is able to control his or her tongue
in the face of insults or uncomplimentary statements."

R. D. Ashe

CHAPTER FOUR

Magnolia Pressure and Influence

A story I have to share,
I HAVE TO...

By
Arlene Bell Peck

Sometimes it's just easier to sit back and keep things to yourself, the good and the bad, that is until you remember why you are here...TO HELP OTHERS. I have talked to many people who figure that their lives don't have meaning and that they don't have anything in their lives worth sharing. Well, I believe that each of us has a story to tell and a song to sing. What is more astounding is that there is always someone out there just waiting to hear your particular story.

Now, that brings me to the events of this past week. I am reminded of just how much we take life for granted. As I sat watching the celebratory anniversary celebration of the historical "March on Washington" that changed the direction of All America, I could not help but remember all the injustices that I personally witnessed growing up in Birmingham, Alabama. What strikes me as being so amazingly astounding is that as a child growing up during the 40's and 50's I innocently assumed a few things were just the normal way of life, so I was fairly comfortable with life as it was then.

I'm talking about the regulations that dictated my place in society at that time: having to sit in the back of the bus; being only allowed to drink from water fountains and use bathroom facilities labeled "Colored," only being able to consider attending a college that admitted Black students because I couldn't even think of being admitted to let's say, The University of Alabama, even though it was located in Tuscaloosa, Alabama just 58 miles from my home in Birmingham. (The irony is that I actually attended Stillman College, a small Black college that was supported by the Presbyterian Church that was also located in Tuscaloosa and most of our faculty was from the University of Alabama)

I'm speaking of a time when being allowed to sit in a section of a lunch counter designated "Colored" in downtown Birmingham;" only associating with and having Black friends because we lived in an all Black neighborhood and our schools and churches were all Black; having to use second hand books at school from the White schools; only being able to attend Black theaters or climb up a fire escape to sit in the balcony of the Lyric Theater because we (Blacks) were not allowed to sit on the main floor; buying hamburgers for my mother and me from a fast food restaurant on Super highway on the way to Bessemer and returning the next day to purchase another one only to be faced with a sign that read, "We don't serve colored here."

At that time it was alright because that was the way it was back then. The sad thing is that I thought that it was normal and the way it was supposed to be. Even though I knew this, I did wonder why some times. They only paid very meager wages, sometimes not enough to put food on our table or pay the rent. I remember that my parents and sisters had to take a test and pay a poll tax in order to vote. And yes, I thought all of these things were also perfectly normal and natural.

It wasn't until the Civil Rights Movement started that I became sensitized to the fact that my family and I actually had the same rights as any other American and did not have to suffer humiliation of subservience in any arena of American life. In fact, when I went off to college I dreamed of becoming a lawyer with the idea that I could effect changes that could help rid "my people" of the injustices that they had endured through the years. But, becoming a lawyer was just not in the cards for me I guess. God obviously had another plan for me.

THE BOMBINGS…Author Shores, the lawyer for Autherine Lucy when she led an attempt to get Black students admitted to The University of Alabama, lived just across town from me. His daughter, Helen and I were girl scouts together. Because of his work in the Civil Rights movement, the Klu Klux Klan bombed his home more than once. Four little girls were killed when 16th Street Baptist Church was bombed. The father of the Robinson girl was my band teacher in elementary school and one of the other families lived in my neighborhood.

THE CROSSES…I remember the crosses that the Klan began to burn all around the city. I remember one night when Steve and I were strolling to the café located across the highway (actually 11E) from Stillman's campus when we noticed a processional of cars and all the occupants in the cars had what looked like white sheets over their heads and faces. At the end of the processional was a truck that had a burning cross on its bed. When they had passed and it was safe for us to cross the highway we walked over to the café' and ordered our bologna sandwiches and the icebox lemon pie, both of which only Mrs. Marshall, who owned and ran the café could make that drew us back again and again. As we were leaving the café' to return to campus, the processional was returning from their venture, having apparently left the burning cross on someone's property. I guess today we would call this a "hate crime."

FEAR...There was an organization in Tuscaloosa called the White Citizens Council that perpetuated racial segregation. One day a suspicious man was seen wondering around the campus. I remember seeing him in our chapel program that morning and later in the library viewing a scale of the campus that was on exhibition there. A little later all students were ordered to be in their dormitories by 9:00 and the entrances to the campus were blockaded. You see there was a Chinese couple, Dr. and Mr. Lo, who taught English and many times they entertained students at their home. It was rumored that the White Citizens Council and/or the Klan was going to pay the Lo's a visit and, fearing that trouble would erupt, the dean took the necessary precautions to keep the student body safe. Everyone was frightened. We had all heard of instances like this, but had never actually experienced anything like this, nor ever imagined that we would.

THE TRIP TO BIRMINGHAM TO MEET WITH MARTIN LUTHER KING ...By this time the bus boycotts had begun. Following my experience of being threatened with having to get off the bus if I did not move to the back, a group of students began to meet to explore how we could organize a boycott in Tuscaloosa. We just needed to know how to go about it. So, one Sunday afternoon Dr. King was speaking at a church in Birmingham very near my home. Mrs. Preswood, one of the cafeteria workers had quite a large car and took several of us to Birmingham hoping to see and hear him and possibly get a chance to meet with him. The plan was that I would remain in Birmingham to meet with him and stay overnight with my parents and have my daddy bring me back to Tuscaloosa the next morning. What is it they say about "the best laid plans of mice and men?"

First of all, when we arrived at the church, the crowd was so huge that there was no thought of getting in. People were crowded around the church just hoping to get a glimpse of Dr. King, but we were at least in ear range to hear him speaking. Next, when we went to my parent's home and told them of our plan, my daddy said, "if you don't get back down to that school as fast as you can you had better." His words still ring in my ears. I was very upset and cried and told him he just didn't understand. Needless to say, and perhaps without knowing it, my father, in his infinite wisdom, actually saved me from danger. You see, that very night The Gadsden Motel where Dr. King and his party were staying was BUMBED, though nobody was killed. It seems that all of my life I have sort of been distanced from all the "action" and perhaps for good reason. Many were killed during "The Movement," and I very well could have been a victim. But I was always wanting and willing to at least do my part. If I were only a part of it, I knew I could and would make a difference. It was sort of like being on the outside looking in. All of the above things, coupled with being a product of poverty were a double whammy.

PRESIDENT JOHNSON…Following the events of the historic Civil Rights March on Washington, President Johnson signed the Civil Rights Bill making segregation of schools and public facilities and transportation illegal. The 50th anniversary of that historic time in history and in my life marks a milestone in American History. While Dr. King's "dream" and vision for a better tomorrow for his children and all children and for all persons to have equal rights as American citizens is still in the making. I am aware that we still have a long way to go until the "dream" has totally become a reality. But, today's scripture gives me hope.

"For I know the plans I have for you, declares the Lord, plans to prosper you and not to harm you, plans to give you hope and a future." (Jeremiah 29:11) The charge we have comes from Proverbs 3:5-6 that admonishes "Trust in the Lord with all your heart and lean not on your own understanding; in all your ways acknowledge Him and, He will make your paths straight."

THIS IS WHY I JUST HAD TO SHARE MY STORY. I hope it blesses and gives hope to someone who might be tempted to lose hope. But, the best is yet to come!

Be blessed today and always and know that I love you as you share your story.

Arlene Bell Peck received the Bachelor Degree from Stillman College, and a Master Degree from the University of Tennessee. She is enrolled in the Doctoral Program at the University of Tennessee.

Woman's Stillman roots run deep—Tuscaloosa News.com

Published: Saturday, October 20, 2012

By

Kim Eaton, Staff writer

(An excerpt)

The wall of her small office was covered with framed certificates and awards received over the years, her bookshelf cluttered with photos of former students. After 45 years at Stillman College, 68-year old Annie Mary Gray has seen it all.

From three or four buildings to a sprawling campus that spreads across 105 acres, Gray has witnessed the growth of the college, as well as the changing trends and attitudes among its students.

"It is interesting to walk around campus now and see how much it has changed, see how much the students have changed," said the Tuscaloosa resident.

Gray's connection to Stillman goes back as far as she can remember. She was born on campus in 1944 in what was then Emily Estes Snedecor Nurses' Training School and Hospital, the only health care facility for black people in West Alabama, Gray said.

She lived 10 blocks away from the school and, after graduating from high school in 1962, she began her college education at Stillman. Her relationship with Stillman continued when she was hired as a faculty secretary after she earned an associate's degree in business administration from C.A Fred Technical College in 1967. She said the key to success is "doing what you're supposed to do and leaving everything else alone."

Her various jobs have allowed her an opportunity to not only witness the changes happening on campus, but to be part of them. Gray also finds comfort in what has not changed. Her birthplace, Snedecor Hall, still stands in the same location. It has been home to the science department and library, and now holds the business school. "It makes me feel really good to see it and remember that's where I was born," Gray said.

A Student's First Impressions

By
Irma Blackburn McConner

The most enjoyable and meaningful years of my life were the ones spent on the campus of Stillman College. I was an eighteen year old very talented and impressionable young lady who had lived in Tuscaloosa all my life under the protection of my parents and seven brothers. However, my excitement about entering college and finally being able to make decisions on my own could be matched with any of the students who came from other cities and states. I felt important and vulnerable, as well as a little fearful knowing that completing college would be a major stepping stone into the next phase of my life.

Orientation and testing was really a breeze for me. I'd always loved school and took achievement very seriously. I scored very high in Math and was encouraged to pursue a math major. However, my big brother "Tree" was a physical education major. I always adored and respected my big brother so I decided to follow suit. College was for me and I was ready for college! Wow, was I ever in store for a rude awakening! It was not an easy task keeping up with a blind math teacher who had an assistant who wrote on the board as he taught. Two sets of eyes were needed for this challenge.

Trying to manage my class schedule and my social life was quite the challenge. You see, I was still hanging out with friends who also entered Stillman from Druid High School. Those visits to the Tigers Grill with Lou (my best friend), studying, and cramming for Dr. Carstarphen's tests became quite a chore for me. Thank God for my innate abilities, discipline, my good sense and my strong desire to always do well which would ultimately get me through my freshman year? Still it was such a joy being a Stillmanite!

As life would have it, my family experienced the untimely death of one of my siblings. The tragedy was too much for me to handle and I left school for a semester and lived in Chicago. That time off from school turned out to be true "growing into a real adult" life experience. However, I returned to dear Stillman with a positive attitude and an even stronger desire to achieve.

<u>Memories of Faculty Members</u>

I joined the Tigeretts dance and drill team and what an enjoyable experience that was! I must give accolades to **Dr. Paul Meacham** for starting this team and selecting me as one of the vivacious dancers who would thrill the crowds who attended the basketball games season after season with our precision moves and sultry jazz dance routines.

When **Dr. Meacham** left Stillman, I had the pleasure of dancing as a tigerett under the direction of **Mr. Joe Boyer,** our new band director. I really loved to dance and this opportunity gave me a chance to show off my skills and talents and I knew one day I would direct a drill team at some time during my teaching career. This actually came into fruition during my career as a physical education teacher in inner city Los Angeles when I organized a 55 member drill team that performed at schools and events throughout the city. I will never forget this knowledgeable and professional man who helped to make my Stillman experience a most enjoyable one. Even today, when I visit Stillman during homecomings, I am recognized as one of Stillman's first tigerettes. It sure makes me pretty proud! What a joy to be a real Stillmanite!

I must mention everybody's hero, Dr. Joffre Whisenton, who was head basketball coach. Whisenton was known for being kind and fair. He was surely my hero when he so kindly allowed me to work in the athletic office as a means of paying my tuition for a semester. Whew! I guess having a big brother (Tree) on the basketball team had its perks. I'm not sure if I ever told Dr. Whisenton how important that assistance was to me. However, if he gets to read **Under the Magnolia Tree**, he will come to understand how much he was appreciated and loved.

It was quite challenging being a health and physical education major. Many thought of this major as non-challenging and just playing games, but one would quickly change his mind if **Dr. Archie Wade** was their instructor. HA! This "no nonsense" man did not play when it came to academics. Gosh, it took some kind of studying to make an "A" in baseball. Who knew? It didn't matter that we went to the same high school and already knew each other well. The structure was now different. He was now the professor and I was the student who had great respect for him and his achievements. Thank you, Dr. Wade! You were a true example of what the rest of us could achieve.

I am so happy that I was educated at Stillman. The professors were "heavy duty" (well versed in their subject matter) and mediocre work was just not an option.

Hail, Oh Hail Stillman!!!

Irma Blackburn McConner received her B.A. degree from Stillman College in 1967; and her MA degree from Pepperdine University in 1977.

Attending Stillman:
a trick or a treat

By
Woodrow M. Parker

By the mid-1950's, an increasing percentage of African Americans in the South began to attend college. In rural Alabama, the message was clear that to improve your life you either had to attend college go north to find employment, or join the military services. The great migration of African Americans from the south to the north is well known. The majority of young African Americans left home to travel north in search of employment or to enlist in military service. Only a few chose to attend college.

Without a family tradition of college attendance, I never imagined or envisioned myself attending college. People who attended college, in my opinion, were middle-class, uppity people who lived on the south side of the creek. (A small stream of water was the dividing line of country folks and city folks). They were usually light skinned people who talked proper and who made the best grades. I lived on the north side of the creek where the poorest people lived on small farms, in small shotgun houses, so called because one could shoot or see straight through the narrow structure if the front door and the back door were opened. Because children from these families were not expected to attend college, they were not encouraged to take the college preparatory class or curriculum. Since placement tests were not conducted in those days, a student's ability was based on his or her socio-economic level or on where the student lived.

I attended the county training school for "Colored" and was assigned classes in shop and vocational agriculture. I never took advanced mathematics, English, or science courses; and one might find it hard to believe, but throughout my twelve years of school, I was never given an assignment to write a single paragraph. I also never took a course in Algebra or Biology. Needless to say, I was not prepared to attend college.

Given my skimpy academic preparation, I was not ready for college. College attendance was not in my DNA. Most of the people in my family had never attended college either. In fact, the only college graduate in our family was an uncle who never talked about his collegiate experience. Some of our relatives said he went to college because he was the member of the family that could not pick at least 200 lbs. of cotton per day. He had been in the military, where he served in World War 11. Like many of the Black veterans, he attended Tuskegee or Alabama State Teachers College where he studied tailoring or some other trade. My uncle was not a role model who would influence me to attend college. Although my parents valued education and encouraged me to reach for the stars where education was concerned, they both dropped out of school early and never had a college or university experience to share.

I had conflicting feelings about attending college. On the one hand, I did not want to spend my whole life picking cotton, picking potatoes, cutting corn, loading watermelons and other kinds of field work. In addition, I did not want to feel jealous of my cousins who's parents could afford to send them to college. My aunt had been a teacher and my uncle was a shrewd business man. Besides, I had heard some of the older Black people say that education turns a person into a "Fool." They also said that people who go to college think that they are better than everybody else. Therefore, I had some feelings of resentment towards Black people from my community who attended college. Like many lower class citizens, my self esteem was too low to applaud those who would seek educational advancement leaving me behind. In essence the "have not's" were always envious of the "haves."

As a student in high school, I placed most of my emphasis on athletics and was not challenged to perform academically. There were several teachers who thought that I was college material, and they often talked to me about attending college. They "just knew" that I was a prototypical college student, but I did not see myself that way at all. I just had some different ideas and plans for my future. In particular, I thought that I would follow the lead of many people who lived in my hometown. After they became old enough, they most often would go to larger cities in the North, East or West. They migrated to Detroit, Chicago, Philadelphia, New York, and many other large cities to find jobs in factories, and anything they could find that would be better than the farm work in rural Alabama. Many of the African American female students would migrate to large cities to work as maids for wealthy white people. Anything was better than slave like labor in the sweltering heat of the summer Alabama sun.

After working up north for several months, they would return home as models of success, driving expensive cars and wearing expensive clothes and jewelry, their symbols of success. In particular, the northern visitors would come home during the Christmas holidays or during the summer and they would parade around town in their new cars, clothes and jewelry for everyone to see. Jimmy Jackson returned from Detroit with suits of every color in the rainbow, wore diamond rings on every finger of his hand, and drove a candy-apple red Ford Thunderbird. We local boys could hardly wait for Jimmy to make his grand appearance. I thought this was much more exciting than going to college. My plan was to follow my older brother who had gone to Detroit and evidently made a great deal of money. I thought that I would graduate and go to Detroit and live with my aunt or my brother for awhile until I could find my own place and get a job in an auto factory and have immediate success and immediate gratification. Then I would return home to display my newfound wealth.

The return of African Americans to my hometown, showing off their cars and their clothes was a tradition that dates back as long as I can remember and was a model for others to follow. Upon their return, these people would tell stories about how wonderful life was in Detroit, Chicago or New York. Not only were there great job opportunities, but there was life with no racial prejudice. It was just the opposite of all the hardship that we faced in our small rural Alabama town, characterized by such hard work as picking cotton, working in the potato fields and working in the corn fields. According to the stories, you would make more than one hundred dollars a day, and you could have all the wonderful things of which a person could dream. This sounded heavenly, because in Alabama, you were lucky to make more than five dollars a day.

So, not only could you make a great deal of money and have nice cars and clothes, but a person was treated with dignity and was treated as a human being, and there was no racism. White people treated black folks with respect, and you could go anywhere you wanted. You could live where you wanted, you could even eat in any restaurants you wanted, and it was not necessary for you to have to go to the back of the bus, or to go to the back of the restaurant. You could go in and sit down among white people and eat a meal. You could even attend school with white people. I had never heard of this —attending school with white people. You could attend school and there was just no racism, according to the stories that they would tell. As I became aware of this world of magic in these northern, eastern or mid-western cities, I certainly did not want to go to college.

I would always present these arguments when my teacher would talk to me about going to college. He'd say, "McClain (my middle name), you ought to go to college. I know Detroit sounds good, but it might not be all that they say it is." I had the proof, I mean, I had seen my brother, who had almost no clothes when he left home to go to Detroit, return with three or four suits, Stacy Adams shoes, Johnson Murphy shoes and Edwin Claps - all of the symbols of success. Not only did he have these nice clothes, but also he had bought himself what was known as a duce and a quarter - a Buick Electra 225. he came back with cars, suits, shoes and hats and a pocket full of money, jewelry, and surely, this was more attractive than going to college.

I had spent many days in the cotton field daydreaming about life in the large cities and how everything was just absolutely perfect.

I would begin thinking about life in the large cities early in the morning as I began to work in the fields. I would often forget that I was in the fields, because I was dreaming about being in the city and returning to Atmore, my hometown, in the nicest car in which anybody had ever returned. What made the car so important was that growing up, there was never a car in my family. My father died when we were young, and my mother carried the total responsibility for our care. Of course, we worked to help ourselves as much as we could, but there was never a car in my family. A car became a symbol of success, and buying a car was even more important to me. Having gone through junior high school and now into senior high school, the moment had finally come for me to go to Detroit to find my fortune. One day during lunch hour, toward the end of my senior year, a young African American instructor, my senior advisor, called me aside and talked with me about my plans.

He said, "Parker, what are you going to do?"

I said, "I don't think you've been listening to me. I've been telling you for the last three years that I plan to go to Detroit and work in an auto factory. And I'm going to show you what I can do when I go up to Detroit, because I'll manage my money well, and I'll come back and show you that it's better to work in the factory than to go to college."

Then he answered, "Since you are so intent on going to Detroit to work, I'd like to make you a proposition. I'd like to buy your ticket to Detroit."

Now he had my attention. He wanted to buy my ticket to Detroit. This sounded really, really interesting because I did not have the money to buy my ticket. However, there was a catch. In order for him to buy my ticket, I had to first go to college for at least two weeks, and if I did not like it, then he would send me a ticket to go on to Detroit. Well, that seemed like a pretty good deal. I could go to college and pretend that I was interested in college for about two weeks. Then I'd give him a call and have him send my ticket. I'd get on the Trailways bus, and then off to Detroit I'd go.

If I attended college, I would encounter two major challenges. The first would be a lack of academic preparation, and the second would be a lack of financial support. Because I was no stranger to hard work and sacrifice, I could overcome the academic deficiencies. The greatest problem would be financial support. Although I explained this dilemma to my teacher, he told me to just give college a chance and I should not worry about financial concerns. He had made a couple of calls to Stillman College to find whatever financial assistance he could get for me. I had never heard of Stillman College, but my advisor said, "Well, you know, Stillman College is a small college with a family-like atmosphere where you will fit nicely; and Stillman is on your route to Detroit." So I packed the few clothes I had and boarded a Trailways Bus to Tuscaloosa, Alabama where Stillman College is located.

It was about 9:00 p.m. when I arrived in this strange place feeling very anxious not knowing where Stillman College was located or how I would fit in. As soon as I stepped off the bus, a cadre of students greeted me, and told me they expected me. They took my bag of clothes and drove me off to Stillman College.

I was pleasantly surprised that this arrangement had been made, because this 200 mile Trailways bus ride was the farthest distance I had ever traveled from home. For these students to welcome me and take me to my dormitory and to my room was incredible. I met the person in charge of the dormitory who also seemed to be expecting me. He took me to my room, and some strange things began to happen to me immediately. I began to feel like I might belong in college.

Shortly after I arrived on campus, a small cadre of students met me and took me over to a social that was being held I went to the social and met other students. I said to a few students, Well, I'm just kind of passing through. I'm not really here to stay," but they would not hear of that. They just embraced me and made me feel as though I belonged; and I began to feel, almost immediately, that I had found my home. This was one of the strangest things that had ever happened to me in my entire life. After many years of rethinking those first few hours at Stillman College, I still do not fully understand the powerful dynamics that impacted me so severely.

Having spent most of my life planning to go to a city and find a job, I felt like my head was being turned around in a very strange way. I suddenly felt that I was where I belonged. It took me several weeks to figure out that I was not about to go anywhere else. I was going to stay at Stillman College. Within a few days, I found a job as a custodial worker in the women's dorm to help pay for tuition, room and board.

One day, when I was walking across campus, I ran into the Dean of Students. He said to me "Well, Parker, how's it going?

I replied, "I'm doing okay."

Then he asked, "Well, did you find a job?"

I said, Yes I did."

Then he asked, "What are you doing?"

I replied, **"I works in the women's dorm."**

The Dean quickly said, "Uh oh, wait a minute Parker. Remember that first person singular, present, has no s on the verb. So remember that now. You're not supposed to say 'I works,' 'I teaches,' and so forth, you may never find a job, and you will be an embarrassment to your family, yourself and to Stillman College."

I realized in that instant that I needed to do something about my speech and about my understanding of the English language. I thought that maybe one way that I could improve my English—speech and English, and at least I would learn how to use the language more effectively than I did at that time. I would never be great at it, but at least I would be able to communicate. The other thing I decided was to take my time, and try and speak correctly, and that seemed to work out okay. I still had a major problem, because the job as a janitor in the dormitory was not sufficient for meeting my financial needs. I had what was called a "C Work Scholarship," meaning that I needed to maintain a "C" average to keep this scholarship. With the scholarship, I could work and have enough money for my tuition, room and board, but I did not have enough money for such necessary things as clothes, toiletries, school supplies or anything else.

My Mother who worked in a laundry most of her life, could not help, because she had six children in the family and only made about sixteen dollars a week. Given this scenario, I needed to find someway to survive. I had decided no matter what, I was going to stick it out, rather than yielding to the temptation of leaving and going to the easy money in Detroit. Although I was poor and needed financial assistance, I was bound and determined to make it, because it seemed I had finally found my home.

Life is difficult on a college campus when you are poor. It is even more difficult when you are teased by fellow students for having so little. I was told I was so poor that I could have brought all of my belongings in one sack. Someone suggested that I paid for my tuition with two pigs from my grandfather's farm. I was able to endure that joking and teasing because I had found the place where I belonged, and the thought of being a college graduate somehow became much more important to me than being able to return home in a nice car, fancy clothes and jewelry. The more they teased me, the more I became determined to "stay the course" until one day I became a college graduate.

By the time I thought I had exhausted all resources for securing additional money, something strange happened to me one Friday night that would positively influence the rest of my college life. I went over to the barber's house for a haircut, but the barber was so intoxicated that he could not cut my hair. When I attempted to leave, another customer came and sat in the barber's chair because he thought that I was the barber. Although I had never cut anybody's hair in my life, I thought, "Why not? I commenced to cut the customer's hair. When I finished, he looked at his haircut in the mirror, nodded his head with approval, and paid me fifty cents for the job. In that moment, I thought of miracles about which my grandparents had talked and sung. This had to be the work of the almighty God, who empowered me with the confidence, faith and skills to cut hair, although I had never cut hair before. My grandparents gave biblical accounts of miracles such as Daniel being saved because God locked the jaws of lions in the lion's den; of God quenching fire in the fiery furnace to save the lives of three men; of David, a shepherd boy, killing the giant with a sling shot; and of Jesus feeding 5,000 people with two fish and five loaves of bread. Perhaps God had one more miracle left, and he gave it to me. Now I say as my grandparents would say often, "Blessed be the name of the Lord."

Before the customer left, he said, "Say, that's not a bad haircut. Thank you. I'd like to come back next Friday for another haircut." While I was excited and content with what I had done, I wasn't sure at the time that I could do it again. These feelings of self-doubt were shortly allayed, because my career as the campus barber took off by leaps and bounds. Fortunately, my barber back home gave me a pair of clippers and the other tools that I needed to get started, and the rest is history. I quickly became the college barber where I not only earned enough money to finance my college education, but also earned enough to help my mother and younger siblings back home. Every now and then, I run into people whose hair I cut while I was at Stillman College, and they introduce me to their friends and family as their college barber. Beginning with that day that I gave that miracle haircut to a stranger, I was never broke again. I always had a few dollars in my pocket.

During my experience as a barber, I began to develop social and communication skills by interacting or communicating with students who were my customers and who came from all regions of the United States and from various international countries. Sometimes I wonder if those days of listening to the problems of students as I cut their hair might have, in some ways, led to my becoming the counselor educator and researcher that I am today.

Richard D. Ashe, Ph.D

One of the most important landmarks in my life was having completed college. This achievement was especially meaningful because attending and completing college was beyond my wildest dreams. I feel fortunate and even lucky that someone, a teacher, identified me as someone who had the intelligence and initiative to succeed in college and in life. While in college, I not only was prepared to make a living, but I learned how to live. In particular, I gained confidence in myself, learned the value of respecting and appreciating others, and learned the value of being a responsible and self-sufficient person.

Throughout my adult life, I have observed hundreds of young people who are lost or confused about their future career directions. Some of them have been a mirror of me before someone stepped up and offered some support and guidance. Many times, I have used my experience in creative ways to help others, as I was helped when I needed it most. This is one way I have been able to repay my teacher, my mentor and my model for improving the quality of my life, even if he had to trick me into attending college. Finally, my introduction to Stillman College was a trick, but terminated as a treat.

Woodrow M. Parker received a B. S. degree from Stillman College, M. S. and Ph.D degrees from the University of Florida.

A Bad Decision in
the Registrar's Office

By
Richard D. Ashe

One of the saddest and surprising times of my Stillman experience was when one of my friends, Calvin Booker (not his real name) made a decision of extreme bad judgment. Calvin, a sophomore from South Alabama had gained quite a reputation on campus for more reason than one. Calvin was viewed by many as extremely intelligent, ambitious and was always well dressed. He was also a participant in extra curricular activities. Some felt that he was destined to become Student Government President.

Calvin was also a work study student whose job was to clean the office suites in the Registrar's Office. Students who were assigned to work study positions in that office were viewed to be highly favored and trustworthy by the administration. During the mid-term examination period, several of Calvin's friends convinced him to change their poor grades to positive grades. His position allowed him to gain access to grades that teachers had turned into the office during the reporting period. Calvin's decision to grant the request of a few students was a rare decision of bad judgment.

A suspicious office worker's observation noticed that some student's grades had been altered. An investigation and inquiry pointed to Calvin Booker. A swift convening of the Student Tribunal Committee found Calvin guilty as charged. The Tribunal Committee also decided to permanently expel Calvin from Stillman College. It appeared that the administration meant to send a clear message to students. "If you make bad choices, you will receive bad results."

Although Calvin Booker's college goals were altered, his intellect allowed him to join the military service and eventually become an officer in the United States Army.

Changes in the Southland

(Preface)

During the final stages of completing **Under the Magnolia Tree,** this author came upon a copy of an interview that was located in an old educational storage file. The interview was conducted by Brooke Brandon White thirteen years earlier. Upon reading the contents of the interview, I began to think that the substance of the questions and answers that were given over a decade ago encompassed historical subject matter that's still relevant for discussion today especially about efforts to suppress minority voting privileges. The information discussed in the interview can help enlighten the awareness of individuals who study American History during the Civil Rights Period and beyond. The interview touches upon a time when southern laws were a painful period in the lives of many African Americans; and how those laws disappeared.

Moreover, my experiences as an African American growing up in the south are not only my experiences, but a realistic depiction of how harsh "Jim Crow Laws" affected thousands and perhaps millions of African Americans growing up in that region of the country. I am honored and delighted that Ms. White chose me as an interviewee to complete one of her college class assignments. Excerpts of that interview report are as follows:

Changes in the Southland
One Man's Experience
(An interview with Dr. Richard Ashe)
By
Brooke Brandon White

Minorities in American History
Oral History
4/14/01

African Americans have a long history of suffering and triumph. They began their struggle in this country as slaves. Although they were freed after the Civil War they still had many chains of oppression and racism to break before they could claim their rights as American citizens. For many years after the period of slavery African Americans lived under the "Jim Crow Laws" which kept them from having the same rights as whites.

Dr. Richard Ashe was born an African American during this time and experienced first hand the burden of segregation. He also experienced the breaking down of this racist system during the Civil Rights Movement of the fifties and sixties.

When slavery was abolished in 1860 the government began restorations in the south. This period, known as Reconstruction, opened up opportunities for African Americans in the political and economic systems (Norrell 1). As time went on however, the southerners began to gain back control of their states. This new gain of control gave them the opportunity to undo the advances that had been made for the African American community. They began to create laws, which segregated African Americans from whites.

These laws included separate bathrooms, schools, eating areas, and transportation. These laws were dubbed the "Jim Crow Laws" and they got this name from a popular minstrel show at the time, which portrayed the African American in a very negative light. African Americans tried to fight these new laws by bringing lawsuits to the courts. In 1896 a lawsuit was brought before the courts concerning the separation of whites and African American on trains. The judge then ruled that segregation was constitutional as long as the facilities provided for both parties were equal. It is this case, Plessy vs. Ferguson, and the ruling of "separate but equal" that gave the "Jim Crow Laws" staying power in the south for many years to come.

It was under these laws that Dr. Richard Ashe was born. He was born in Marion, North Carolina; a small town he says many have referred to as a "one horse town." He refers to it as "God's country" because of its beauty and pleasant climate. It was here in God's country" that Ashe felt the sting of segregation. Dr. Ashe says about the experience "When I think of the times growing up as a youngster they were delightful times and at the same time they were very painful." Ashe remembers during his school years they received white students' used books. Also they did not have bus services provided for them so they walked by the white school everyday. Ashe remarks however

"...that was just a way of life. You didn't bother thinking whether it was right or whether it was wrong...it was painful being treated like a second-class citizen but at the time that was the way it was and that was accepted. That was the way it was for many, many years."

The unequal treatment of African Americans in public life led many of them to believe that they were, in fact, unequal or inferior to the white race. They had been born into a system of inequality and for many of them it was all that they knew. "I remember having what we call a mind set or a "brain set" that we were not as good as white people," says Ashe. He continues to say, "many did not like our skin color...we detested the way our hair looked...we didn't like our thick lips and our wide noses...Many of us didn't like ourselves."

While Dr. Ashe was beginning to work on his bachelor's degree in English at Stillman College in Tuscaloosa, Alabama, the Civil Rights Movement was becoming a powerful force for change in the ways African Americans were treated. By this time Brown vs. The Board of Education (1954) had banned segregation in schools, Rosa Parks had been arrested and the bus boycott had brought about integrated bus systems in Alabama (1955-56), and the sit-in movement at Woolworths in Greensboro, North Carolina by four black college students had started a nationwide protest against segregated lunch counters (1960) (Blakeman 1). One change that Dr. Ashe witnessed firsthand was the change in the south from segregated sports to integrated sports. He states: "There was football and there was Paul "Bear" Bryant. They worshipped the man in Alabama. He won National Football Championships year after year and there were no black football players on his teams. Then they played the University of Southern California and I attended that game.

Even though Alabama was my home team I was pulling for U.S C. because I saw this as an historic moment. It was a defining time. A player by the name of Sam "The Bam" Cunningham ran all over Alabama's team. As a result of that humiliating defeat Paul "Bear" Bryant said "I'm going to get me a black ball player." That's what started it. Alabama did it and then all of a sudden the other southern teams had no problem with it. I was at that game." As the segregation laws of the south began to fall apart African Americans began to exercise their long awaited freedoms. "As a result of the laws...we began to enjoy the rights of citizens...Going to a restaurant was wonderful. You could go into a restroom and you weren't using one based on race. Being able to go on an overnight trip and ... knowing you could rest your weary body. That was a dramatic change."

While growing up in North Carolina one thing that was instilled in Ashe was the importance of a good education. One of the main factors that inspired Ashe to seek out a good education was the workers he would see coming home every night from the mill in his town. Many of his own friends he says "waited until they were sixteen so they could quit school and work at the mill because that's all they saw." However, Ashe says of the workers, "I saw how they looked when they got off from work and I said that's not for me." Because of this desire to receive a good education Ashe went on from Stillman College to receive his Master's degree from Indiana University, a Specialist degree at the University of Alabama, and finally his Ph.D in Administration from The University of Minnesota. He says of his Ph.D: "The proudest moment of my life was the day that I received my Ph.D degree. I was so proud because of the trials and tribulations that I had. It seems like there was just roadblock after roadblock, adversity after adversity. When I think of the inferior education that

I got in that, small town, compared to white students and then being able to obtain the highest degree that educational institutions bestow was a proud moment." I accepted the Ph.D on behalf of my family and friends of Marion, N. C.

Dr. Ashe still continues to believe in the educational system as "the key to success" and tries to instill this in the students he works with as the assistant principal of a Clayton County School. He wants his students to realize that "The opportunities at one time were not opened for us" and his wish is that they take "advantage of the opportunities they now have." Ashe's position in school systems over the years allowed him to witness change in the way students feel about themselves and in relation with others. Ashe refers to his lack of self-esteem growing up when he says "I have seen those types of feelings disappear over the years with the students I have taught. They feel comfortable in the classroom with anybody ... in terms of who they are race wise. However, the psychological damage and brainwashing of the minds of African Americans for hundreds of years isn't something that can be easily erased."

Dr. Richard was born in North Carolina at a time when segregation was a way of life for those in the south. As he grew into a young man he witnessed this country change its laws and he witnessed, "Attitudes that change hearts." He has felt the change of feeling like a "second-class citizen" to feeling comfortable enough to say, "I'm Black and I'm Proud."

As an educator he has seen the differences that changes have made from generation to the next in this country. He uses his life to give back to others and help instill in the young generation of today the values that were instilled in him.

Dr. Richard Ashe is the author of several books. These books include Poetic Expressions, Morning Time, and Soulful Poetry. Many of the poems in these books were inspired by Dr. Ashe's experiences as a young man growing up in the segregated south.

Works Cited

Blakeman, Andrew. "The Civil Rights Movement: Timeline." **Black Rights lin the U.S.A.** 1(1998): Oneline.

http://members.tripod.com/-ablakeman/1.htm

Norrell, Robert J. "The Civil Rights Movement in the United States." Microsoft @Online Encyclopedia 2000 http://encarta.msn. com 1997-2000 Microsoft Corporation.

Interview With Dr. Richard Ashe
By
Brooke Brandon White

(Interview Excerpts)

Brooke Brandon White

Minorities In American History

3/12/01

Person I've chosen to interview: Dr. Richard Ashe

Minority Group: African American

Age: 53

Occupation: Assistant Principal for the Clayton County Alternative School

- Questions -

White - Please give me some background information about you first and then we will proceed with the questions that I have prepared.

Ashe - You won't have the time (laugh). I'm a native of Marion, North Carolina. That's thirty-six miles from Asheville, North Carolina. A very, very small town. Many used to refer to it as a "one horse town" (laughs). That is also eighty four miles from Charlotte, North Carolina. We call Marion and the surrounding area "God's Country" because of its beauty and pleasant climate. That is where I completed my elementary and high school education.

From there I went to Stillman College, that's in Tuscaloosa, Alabama and there I received my Bachelor's degree in English with a minor in Social Studies. After that I returned to Marion, North Carolina for approximately one year and got married. We then decided to move to Alabama and I worked there at a school called Druid High School. A couple of years later I attended Indiana University and obtained a Masters Degree in 1966. Upon the completion of that degree, I was offered a position at my Alma mater, Stillman College to work in a special program called the College Education Achievement Project. I worked there as an instructor for two years. I left Stillman to accept an administrative position at the Board of Education in Tuskegee, Alabama. Prior to going there I obtained a Specialist Degree from the University of Alabama.

I then moved to Minnesota where I received my Ph.D from the University of Minnesota. My family and I stayed there for approximately fifteen years. Over the years, my family kept encouraging me to move back south. They wanted to go home. I tried to tell them at that time that we were already at home and they continued to say "No. We are not at home. We want to go south. We want to go home." When they gave me a date and said (my wife and daughter) "Now this is the deadline - the date that we're going home and if you want to go home with us - fine!" I knew they were serious then. So I started looking for a centrally located area. My home in North Carolina and my wife's home being in Alabama.

Atlanta was the perfect spot. The interesting thing about Atlanta was that I had said many times that it was one city I would never live in. The traffic basically terrified me. But once coming to Georgia, I had the opportunity to teach in Dekalb County. Later, I accepted an administrative position in nearby Clayton County.

White - Well that was a very in-depth history. You've been all over (both laugh).

White - My first question is how has being a part of a minority group in America change in your lifetime and how has it remained the same?

Ashe - The interesting thing about the history of being an African American and as old as I am, I have seen a lot of changes. The history, although it's a very painful history, at the same time is full of opportunities and accomplishments. When I think of the times growing up as a youngster they were delightful times and at the same time they were very painful. Those experiences later allowed me to put them into poetry. What comes to mind is when black kids weren't allowed to play in a park that was on the edge of our community. As a youngster, I recall going into the park and asked a question to an obvious answer. The answer and reception that I received was quite shocking to me. The experience that I had, I crafted into a poem, "Can Colored Kids Play in This Park? **(Poetic Experessions)** It was also a time when individual races did not mingle - that was taboo - that was simply against the law.

Another thing that was painful was receiving the hand me down books that the white students had used. Also, I lived in a neighborhood where I walked to school. There was no bus service provided for us, and so we walked and passed the white school.

That was just a way of life. You didn't bother about thinking whether it was right or whether it was wrong. Your mind set was "This is the way things are."

Richard D. Ashe, Ph.D

The sixties was during the height of black consciousness. When James Brown's song came out "I'm Black and I'm Proud" and during that time period the bus boycott in Montgomery and the sit-ins that began in Greensboro, North Carolina, just sort of spread throughout the south. So as a result of these events, I saw laws change. The attitudes of individuals, white as well as African Americans, changed.

I also remember having what we call, a "mind set" [or a] "brain set" that you are not as good as white people and so I am reminded of the time when many of us didn't like our skin color; or the way our hair looked. So we straightened or processed it. Many of us didn't like our thick lips and wide noses. As a result of the sixties that all changed. We were black and we were proud.

I want to get back to the skin color. This is something I'm going to share with you that was within the black community. Again, some of us were prejudice and very conscious about skin color. I'm reminded of a little cliché:

"If you're black - get back.
If you're brown stay around
If you're yellow [high yellow black] – you're mellow.
If you're white - you're all right."

So if you were light skinned you were okay and you had certain types of privileges as a result of skin color. So here again, that was then but this is now.

Because of the Civil Rights laws a lot of opportunities opened up for African Americans in all aspects of life, especially in politics. I

166

recall when Adam Clayton Powell, you may not recall him – may not of even heard of him - but he was the sole African American in the United States Congress. At that time he represented, not just a New York district, he represented all black Americans and he was looked at with pride. The voting rights bill changed opportunities dramatically for African Americans in the South. I never encountered a voting problem in North Carolina but there were incidents in Georgia and in Alabama. We also had the denial of opportunities in Mississippi.

I will never forget another change that I witnessed. That was segregated sports. There was football and there was Paul "Bear" Bryant. They worshipped the man in Alabama. He won national championships year after year without black players. They played U.S.C., the University of Southern California. I attended that game. U.S.C. was a powerhouse and so was the University of Alabama.

Even though Alabama was my home team I was pulling for U.S.C. because I saw that as an historic moment; it was a defining time. A player by the name of Sam Cunningham, and they called him "Sam the Bam Cunningham" ran all over Alabama's team. As a result of that humiliating defeat "Paul "Bear" Bryant said I'm going to get me a black ball player. He said I'm going to integrate my team. That's what started it. Alabama integrated its football team and all of a sudden other teams in the south had no problem with it. I was at that game and had the privilege of witnessing a defining time in sports history.

It saddens me to see now where the opportunities at one time were not opened up for us and then see where many youngsters are not taking advantage of the opportunities that they [now] have. Education is the key to success. It can open up doors; unforeseen doors. Many of these students don't seem to realize this and it's unfortunate that they will not realize the opportunities that they had while they were in school.

White - In what ways do the younger generation relate with each other that has stayed the same? Are the prejudices still at the forefront?

Ashe-They are definitely not at the forefront. The prejudices are very subtle. When I'm talking about prejudices I'm not only talking about prejudice from white people but black people as well. Many people don't like to talk about their prejudices because that's dear; you're talking about one's own being. They don't want to be accused of being a racist. You're talking about body, soul and spirit but there's a willingness now to cooperate with each other in order to do the best that you possibly can over situations.

At one time there was an overwhelming resistance to the integrating of schools by teachers. White teachers did not want to teach black students and then there were [black] teachers who did not want to teach white students. They just didn't want to leave their comfort level. I've seen that change. Then there is the old touchy. You don't see it too much here in Clayton County. I'm speaking of white students dating black students and black students dating white students. I'm of the opinion that - that's one of the things that prevented integration from taking place sooner. Many folks just didn't want their sons and daughters mixing with the opposite race.

White - You talked about the Black Pride movement earlier. What impact has that pride had on your children and future generations? Is that pride stronger or are there still pride issues?

Ashe - There's no doubt about it. My children do not have that lack of self-esteem that I had. I had a lack of self-esteem for years. I felt that I was not good enough and I felt that my place was always in the back. I felt that I was not supposed to be in the front. Others were supposed to be out front. That's not an issue with my kids or for me today. They feel comfortable wherever they are. They feel good about themselves when relating to any one else.

I have seen those types of feelings disappear over the years with the students I have taught. They feel comfortable in the classroom with anybody. Sometimes they may not feel comfortable in a classroom because of the material being taught but in terms of who they are race wise they feel just as comfortable being with anybody regardless to whether its black, white, Hispanic, or Asian.

White-So you think that as a teacher and administrator that's given you a window to see the change from generation to generation?

Ashe - Oh yes.

White - In what way was your life different from that of your children? To what do you attribute these differences?

Ashe - There are light years differences from my upbringing and their [his children] upbringing. I was a product of a large family. So we relied on hand me downs. The interesting thing about growing up, I knew we didn't have a lot but it never crossed our minds that we were poor. We were content. Our family members loved each other and we helped each other. We didn't have much. The clothes that I wore were sometimes shabby looking. The boys' shoes were passed down and worn until the soles and heels were worn out. I remember putting pieces of cardboard box material inside the sole of my shoes to keep rocks from hurting my feet. That's laughable but it's true. That all changed for me when I got a job as a bellhop at the local hotel.

White - Was that hotel segregated? What was your experience there?

Dr. Ashe then began to relate this story to me. The hotel was strictly segregated. At one point while he was working there a new white girl was employed. One night she was teasing him about dancing. She told him she was going to bring a radio the next night and dance with him. He dreaded this. He felt trapped because he knew he would get in trouble for dancing with her but he had also been taught to never refuse the request/demand of a white person. The next day his fear was realized when she arrived with a radio and insisted on dancing with him. He did and said that he noticed raised eyebrows around the room. After that experience he never saw the girl at work again.

He said he never thought about it until he was older and realized that she was fired because she danced with him. He later wrote a poem about his experience entitled "Dancing With Blue Eyes" that appears in his book-<u>Poetic Expressions.</u>

White - Tell me about your poetry.

Ashe - I tried to do several things with my poetry. It was basically something that I always wanted to do. I wanted to leave something behind. I guess its maybe an ego thing but I just wanted to make a mark some way some how. I'm still searching for a a way to make a meaningful contribution. Writing motivational poetry has been an inspirational outlet for me. I also get a kick out of writing poetry with a humorous slant; and of experiences that I have had.

White - When did you begin your poetry?

Ashe-Well the interesting thing about it is I caught pneumonia about six or seven years ago. I could barely move my hand. I could just barley move my body. I was aching all over and I thought I was going to die. That scared me. I was thinking that I'm going to die and not have the opportunity to write anything before leaving this world. So in the middle of the night I had flashbacks of experiences that I had as a youngster as described in "Can Colored Kids Play in This Park" and "Dancing With Blue Eyes". I also remembered the individuals who worked at the local mill. I recalled how sympathetic I was for the tired mill workers when they got off work. At that time I decided that the mill was not for me. I said let me use my brain power not my muscular power to make a living. I guess that's when I started paying a little more attention to my high school studies because I did not want to go to the mill.

White - Did you know individuals who worked at the mill?

Ashe - Yes, I did. In my book Poetic Expressions the poem [I wrote about it] is called "The Power of the Mill." The youngsters, my friends, that's what many wanted to do. They waited until they were 16 years old when they could quit school and work at the mill because that's all they saw. They wanted the money because they wanted good wages in order to purchase an automobile. But I saw how they looked when they got off of work and I said that's not for me. As a result of the flashbacks of those experiences I decided to write. I forced myself to get up from my bed. Although weakened with pneumonia I began to construct poems about my childhood experiences. Before I knew it I had about 17 or 18 poems.

White - What are some specific things you learned from your family that have influenced you?

Ashe - My parents and grandmother continued to impress upon us to live in a way to be respected and to always give respect. She told us to go to school; treat people with kindness; and treat them with dignity. As a result of my parent's and grandmother's rules and expectations, I taught my children to have those same standards. My motivational poems were partly inspired by my family's teachings.

White - Do you think there are still negative attitudes towards race relations in existence today?

Ashe – Oh, there's no doubt about it. Let's take what happened recently in Georgia regarding the state flag. To a lot of students that I taught, the Georgia Flag didn't mean a thing. Some of the younger generation didn't know about the power of symbols. People generally can relate to symbols because they send a strong message that can become influential. A lot of folks don't understand why there was a great effort to change the flag. When you think about why the Civil War was fought in the first place, it was to try to free the slaves, to free our fore parents. African Americans see that Confederate symbol as a "In your face message." We see it as pain and hatred. A lot of people will say "That's part of our heritage." But we see it as something else. Thank goodness that Georgia has done the right thing and changed the state flag. Attitudes change hearts.

White - What do you think about the importance of Black History Month? When you were growing up what did you learn about the importance of black history?

Ashe - In black schools you learned about black history. Teachers made sure we learned about our heroes and the sheroes. It was Black Week. Then when schools were integrated it was side tracked. It was side tracked because there was not a big push to continue this tradition. Later on it became Black History Month. There was a consciousness to learn about black people who helped to make America great. So our schools and the press picked up on it. The interesting thing about it now is that when schools do not choose to observe it there's a backlash.

The fact of the matter is that black history is part of American history and even though part of it is painful it still is history. The Jewish people have Passover and do not allow us to forget the Holocaust. Thank goodness the Clayton County Board of Education here in Georgia has set a standard that the schools are expected to recognize during Black History Month and are held accountable. We live in a society where there are not only black and white but also Hispanic and Asian students. Their history needs to be recognized as well.

White - What was your experience with integration like?

Ashe - Let's talk about the segregation aspect first. Try to put yourself in a position where you are in a public facility and you have two water fountains one labeled white and the other labeled colored. Go to a restaurant that requires you to go around to the back to be served. Then if you are going to travel in the south you know you have to get in the back on public transportation. That was painful being treated like a second-class citizen. But at the time that was the way it was and that was accepted.

That was the way it was for many many years. During the Civil Rights Movement many African Americans began saying we need to have our rights as American citizens. As a result of demonstrations, protests, laws and law suits won, slowly and surely we began to enjoy the rights as citizens. We had opportunities. We could go to a restaurant and not be treated differently based on race. There was the opportunity to be able to go on an overnight trip and not worry about sleeping in your car. You could check into a hotel or motel and rest your weary body. That was a dramatic change.

White - Were you comfortable with that change right away?

Ashe-Well, whenever it came about we were very careful as to where we would go and test this new right that we had. There were individuals who were determined to see no change. There was the attitude, "I don't care what the Supreme Court has said, your place is over there." So gradually you would see individuals able to go to restaurants, restrooms and hotels and I fell right in there and felt comfortable with it as well.

White - What is something that you feel is important for the younger generations to have?

Ashe-The idea of a good education was ingrained in us growing up. At the same time let's not forget who's in charge of everything. Almighty God. So, religion plays a very important part. Go to church or some other religious institution; and be determined to put sunshine in somebody's life through word or through deed. Dedicate yourself to give of your time, talent and your resources.

White - What was your most vulnerable moment as an African American male and your proudest?

Ashe - I think about being in N. C. and in our small town. You're vulnerable with the police. A lot of people think there is an abundance of police brutality and mistreatment of blacks. I can say it's been real for me. You could be stopped day or night. For instance, I've been driving or riding as a passenger when police officers have come up and started harassing you for no reason at all. I've experienced this in Alabama and in North Carolina. They now call it racial profiling. There's nothing you can say or do. However, history has shown that the best things for young African American males to do is use common sense and say yes sir and no sir; and pray that everything is going to be okay. So, that's being vulnerable.

The proudest moment of my life was the day that I received my Ph.D. I was so proud because of the trials and tribulations that I had. It seemed like there was roadblock after roadblock, adversity after adversity. When I think of the inferior education that I got in comparison to the white kids in my small town; and then be able to obtain the highest degree that educational institutions bestow was a proud moment. In a sense, it is also a testament to the great job that our teachers had done. Teachers like Bessie Greenlee, Howard Miller, Margaret Greenlee and Coach Raymond Washington who utilized the resources that they had at their disposal to teach children.

Brooke Brandon White is a graduate from the University of Mississippi.

Unforgettable Night at the Ant Motel

By
Richard D. Ashe

During my senior year at Stillman after the Christmas holidays, I discovered that I had arrived a day earlier than the reopening of the men's dormitory at John Knox Hall. This miscalculation of time forced me to have the taxi driver take me to a local inexpensive motel. The two week holiday season allowed me to work with a food caterer and make some extra spending money. Therefore, the ability to pay for motel accommodations was not an issue.

With time on my hand I decided to call Ella Johnson, (not her real name) a recent graduate of Stillman and take her up on an earlier offer to take me out to dinner. Ella was considered to be in the upper middle class financial status. Ella indicated that she would pick me up around six o'clock. In the meantime, I took a shower and watched television. At approximately six o'clock, Ella was knocking at my motel room door.

I opened the door and invited her to come in for a few minutes before going out to dinner. She agreed. Before sitting down, I noticed Ella's eyes opening wide and looking toward the head of the bed. There was a long line of ants crawling from the floor toward the pillows. Quickly, I threw back the top bed cover and we both were horrified to see hundreds of ants covering a half eaten stale pizza. Ants were all over the bed. Without saying a word, Ella ran to her car and left. I wondered how it was possible for anyone to forget a half eaten pizza under the bed covers in a motel room.

I immediately went to the motel desk and requested another room. The clerk complied and indicated that there would be no charge for the room. That was my first and last date with Ella. We never communicated again.

Three Incredible Staff Members

By

Richard D. Ashe

Looking back over my freshman year's experience, there were three staff members that come to mind. The first is Dr. Joffre Whisenton.

Dr. Whisenton wore at least "three different hats" as a staff member. He was the Men's Dormitory Director, a teacher, basketball coach, and track and field coach. His good advice and excellent teaching methods were incorporated into my teaching style.

The second Stillman staff member who I will always remember is Mr. Paul Meacham. Mr. Meacham was the band director, and administrator of the Work-study Program. When I went to his office to be interviewed for a work-study position, his comments to me were, **"I can give you a job, but I can't keep it for you."** To me, that was a profound statement. Years later, I found myself using his words when I became an administrator.

During the course of numerous discussions with alumni members about Stillman staff who played a major role in their college experience, the name Paul Meacham is usually mentioned.

The third person I choose to mention is the Dean of Students, Ms. Louise Mckinney. From day one at Stillman, freshmen students were told by upperclassmen, "Whatever you do, try to keep from having to go to the Dean of Students Office. They were emphatic in saying "If you go to her office, no good will come from it." I heard this over and over again.

I am truly sorry to make this comparison, but it's the truth. When I saw her on campus, she reminded me of police officers parked on the side of busy highways waiting to stop unsuspected speeding motorist to give them a traffic ticket. One morning during the first semester of our weekly assembly programs, I noticed Ms. Mckinney staring at me. I saw her staring at me at least three different times. I became very uneasy because of her reputation of sending students home for not following school rules.

Three days later, I received a letter addressed to me from the Dean of Students Office. It was a letter from Ms. Mckinney to report to her office on the following Monday. My roommate, Max Parker and I were puzzled as to why I would be receiving such request.

Needless to say, my whole weekend was ruined due to Ms. McKinney's request. I knew that somehow I was going to be on the receiving end of some bad news.

That Monday when I entered Ms. Mckinney's office, I was very nervous. It probably showed on my face. She asked me to please have a seat. For at least 20 seconds, she stared at me without saying a word. Then she said, "How can I help you? I immediately pulled her letter to me from my pocket and handed it to her. She read it, smiled and said "I don't remember why I sent for you." She asked if I had been behaving myself. I assured her that I had. At that point, she said to me with another smile, "Mr. Ashe, have a good day."

Leaving her office was like having a ton of bricks lifted from my shoulders. I was relieved that the trauma that she had put me through was over. I dismissed the unpleasant experience from my mind and chose not to recall it to memory until decades later. The egotistical part of my mind finally helped me to realize why she had requested to see me.

MAGNOLIA SPECIALS

"It's not so much about the disrespect that you receive, but how you respond to the disrespect."

R. D. Ashe

CHAPTER FIVE

Magnolia Specials

(Preface)

After having the privilege of hearing Pinkney Mosley's presentation at the Golden Years Ministry of Elizabeth Baptist Church, Atlanta, Georgia, this author arranged to have him give the same presentation to the "Men's Healthy Living Class" at the Quality Living Service Center in Atlanta, Georgia.

Although Pinkney Mosley is not a Stillman alumnus, his remarkable experiences could be inspirational for readers at every educational and motivational level. Specifically, the challenges he gives in his lecture are appropriate for students, teachers, parents and senior citizens. Below are excerpts of his presentation:

A Pilot's Incredible Experiences

(Overcoming Great Odds)
By
Pinkney Mosley

Good morning gentlemen. It is indeed an honor and pleasure to be invited to speak to you this morning and share with you some of my experiences as a pilot.

Growing up in the forties and fifties in South Carolina and Georgia, my father always told me to learn everything you can. He said, "Learn something new every day." And it doesn't make any difference whether you're 10 years old or 100 years old. "Try to learn one thing every day that you didn't know the day before." So I took the advice to heart and tried to learn how to do a lot of things which helped me throughout my college experience.

At Benedict College in my freshman year (1964), there were civil rights demonstrations. I was right there in the middle of it. Somebody said go, so I did. This was my first experience of being in jail. I can remember one thing and one thing only. There was a man in there that came up to me and said, "I tell you what, you don't have no ladies in here do you?" He said, "Come over here. I didn't know what he wanted because I'm 18 years old and I've never been to jail before. He said, "You got two dollars? I got my lady over here." I said, what you mean, ain't nothing but men in here. I looked over in the corner and saw a guy with his hair all slicked back. He was smiling and going on. I said, oh my goodness, no man, leave me alone!

The second time we got arrested, how things changed. They put us all on a shooting range. All of us college kids were together because they arrested us every time we would sit. But that was back in the sixties and you learn a lot when you're young like that, especially when you're going through things. I was in a mathematics class and the teacher was a Cuban. I will never forget her name and she taught analytical geometry. She was mean to the point that if you didn't have your homework, you couldn't come in class. I was over in the dining hall one morning and somebody asked, "Do you have Dr.Balea's homework? I said, "no, I don't have it." He said well, you know you aren't going to be allowed into class.

Oh my goodness that was in my major. He said if you go down to the student union building and take a test for the Air Force the Dean will excuse you from all your classes today. I said, "That's the ticket. That's exactly what I'm going to do." I went down to take the test and I really didn't care anything about it or what kind of grade I made. I finished the test and gave it back to the test examiner. He said, "You know you have about two hours more." I said, man I'm finished, I'm finished. Well, I had my pass so I didn't have to go to class that day and that's all I wanted.

After he came back about a month later, he said you passed to go to navigator training or pilot training whaever you want to. I said yeah? He said yeah. He said I'm going to take you down to Sumter Air Force Base to get a physical. Well, I didn't answer him because I still hadn't planned on going. So, the man said listen, if I pick you up, would you go down there and take this test? I said well alright. This is just how God works and how you can fall into something without even planning for it.

I went down there and the first thing I did was take an eye examination. He informed me that I was 20/10 in one eye and 20/12 in the other. I said now wait a minute, here they go starting something. I knew they were going to find something wrong with me. I said; now listen, I know I can see. I know I'm 20/20. He said, "Son, I'm trying to tell you, 20/10 is about the best the human eye can get, and you're seeing at 20/10 and 20/12, nobody can see any better." I kind of felt ashamed because I didn't want any mess.

First of all, I had to enlist in the Air Force. I had to enlist because at that time they had the draft. I went down to see a little lady at the Registration Office. Her name was Ruby Dee Trice. I will never forget because she had polio. One of her arms was kind of drawn up. You would see people like that then but you don't see them like that now. But anyway, I went down there to see Ruby Dee Trice. I will never forget her. I said, "I got my papers to go to the Air Force and everything, but I'm not going till November." She said, "We got a problem!" I said, "What do you mean? She said, "If you're not down in Fort Jackson by July 6th or 7th the MP's are going to be looking for you." I will never forget when I walked out of that office, I spoke some words I regret saying. I said I wish her arm would draw up to match that other one.

I went on to basic training and before time they put me in officer training school. I finished all of that and it's a funny thing about meeting people. I met Col John Glenn. Do you remember when he was in the astronaut program? He spoke at our graduation. I left there and came down to of all places, the State of Georgia. We were still back in 1964 and I was down in Valdosta, Georgia at a little Air Force Base called Moody Air Force Base. When I got down there, I was the only one in pilot training. As a matter of fact, I was the only black officer on the entire base. So you got to understand, we started with about 49 people in our class. We finished with about 29.

I was in a group where all kinds of things happened to me while I was down there.

I can tell you many stories, just for being the color that I am. They would send me out on a weather ship as the first one. They would give me lessons I hadn't studied yet. I said well I'm going to make it one way or another. One young man was from Georgia. After about six months, he finally came up to me and said, you know, you're not a bad person, you're alright. I said thank you. But really, I was alright before you gave me your seal of approval.

There are many things that you go through in life, but you should never let anything get you down. Even at this age, we have issues with our health more than anything else, but you still don't let it get you down. I had one instructor, Major Brown, who said, you are going to flunk this class. It was the class for T38 engineers. They were grading on what they called a perfect curve. If everybody else made 100 and you made 85, you just flunked the test. After the test was over, they came out and said five people had flunked the test. I knew I hadn't flunked the test and I went back to him, because this is the only way you can get back at people sometimes. I said Major Brown you know I should have listened when you were talking to me. I've messed around and flunked this test, but if you just help me out a little bit, maybe I could pass it the next time. He kind of swallowed a little bit and looked at me and said, "Well you weren't one of the ones who failed." I said, No kidding! Major Brown, you're a better teacher than you thought you were. You got me through this test. Little things like that would always try to stop you.

I will never forget, I had a check ride with the base commander one day. He was in navigation and he had been a reconnaissance pilot. That's the one that flies low and go a lot of places taking pictures and everything. I said I'm either going to do good with this guy or I'm not. When you're flying like that you have your strip map on your thigh looking at because it's all visual flight routes. (vfr) I had marked down when I would get to my turning points (tps) to target. I said, "I'm going to start counting down and when I get down to zero I'm going to be right over the top of this little bridge out there." I flew the mission and when I got to my tp's, I started counting down because I had to make sure we get to that bridge. I'm either going to do good or I'm going to look bad. We were only about 100 feet off the ground doing about 400 or 500 mph. The T38 was a supersonic trainer. It could go faster than the speed of sound, even though we were nothing but trainees. So I started counting down and when I got down to one, I flipped that T38 over and when I got down to zero, the colonel was looking straight down and there was the bridge right under us. When we got back to base, he kind of let the word go around "Leave him alone." I said, "Just leave him alone."

There was a guy named Mills and we were the first two guys who finished in our class. As a matter of fact, we finished about a month ahead of time and the only thing we had to do was just play around until our graduation. But like I said some things are planned in a higher role than what we are. I left there and went to advanced training at MacDill Air Force Base. That's where I went through F4C training. (Fighter Plane Training)

In the meantime, that's where I met a lot of the guys. I don't know if you remember the Tuskegee Airmen? I knew a lot of them. The guy in the movie that flew the President's wife, Eleanor Roosevelt, wasn't really in the service. He was a civilian that took her up that day. He said the service guys were running around trying to find a phone to call back to the White House because she couldn't get in the plane with this black guy. She said "I'm going to get in." She flew with who we called "Chief." When she got back, she said "wait a minute. You know, you can fly this airplane." He said, "thank you ma'am." She called back to the White House and said "Listen, we got to get this program started." I don't know if you knew the significance, but they called it the "Tuskegee Experiment." They didn't say it was a school or anything. They called it an experiment. You know when they say experiment, it's because we don't know whether it's going to work or not and that's what they thought about the program. I'll have to tell you about all the guys because they were special guys. They went through a lot but they were not appreciated for the things that they did.

But believe it or not, when I got to Delta Airlines, I ran into an old captain. I was flying co-pilot for him. He said, "Moe," (that's my nickname) I was flying on a mission to Berlin, we got what we call a combat frequency center. A wide open frequency center where everybody can listen in on and he heard these guys talking. He was from the state of Georgia and he recognized that they were both of our color. He called and said, "Hey! What you guys doing?" They said their mission was cancelled and were headed back to the base. He said "listen, we're going over to Berlin; will you guys help us get there?" This was in 1937. He said when those Red Tails popped up aside him; he felt so good and never felt better in his life. But this was the job that they did. They hardly ever lost an airplane to enemy violence when they were flying.

I was at a luncheon in New York. Atkins, they said was the first black man to be an Ace Pilot. He shot down one of their PTU's which was a jet airplane. They asked him how did he shoot him down. He said, I just pulled the trigger ahead of him and he flew right into the bullets. But he did do that. Those guys were wonderful.

When I went to Delta Airlines there were three of us. After five years, there still were only four blacks. Right now it's still about as bad. We only have about ½ of one percent professional pilots that are of us. All the times when they're doing things like this; God will put someone in your path to help you out. I will never forget when I had a check ride with the captain. I was flying co-pilot and he just couldn't fly the airplane. It was just a new little plane he'd just flunked out. He said "I'm quitting." I said, "What do you mean?" He said "I'm quitting. I told my wife before I left, if I got into any trouble I was just quitting. I've got enough time for retirement." So he said let's get out of the airplane. The guy said to some other pilots, "Moe is taking his check ride, why don't you finish helping him" "No," he was told. He has got to go too. Anytime you go out and don't complete a ride, they eventually take your license away from you. So you come back in for a day of training and they'll return your license.

I never will forget this guy. He tried coming in to talk with me. I said, "I really don't want to talk to you right now, I'm doing my retraining." I went through my retraining and when I had my debriefing, the guy said, "I don't see what the matter is. Technically, you flew that ride a lot better than I did." But these are the kind of things you run into.

There was a guy we called him Mr. Delta. I can't call his name right now, but he told me when I flew with him on my first night in Atlanta. He said, Moe, don't let anybody tell you that you can't fly this airplane. He said, I've flown with many guys and I'm an experienced pilot. He was two years from retiring. Don't ever think that someone's going to say that you can't fly an airplane. This is the kind of encouragement that helped you, and it helped me out for a long time because I knew I could do the job. When I went through all the training and everything else and flew all kinds of aircraft it was good and it was a lot of fun, but when I went to Vietnam that wasn't any fun.

I flew 171 missions; a lot of them were over Hanoi. We used to call them a round pack of sticks. If we flew enough of them over there, then sooner or later they were going to catch you. I flew about sixty of them over Hanoi, and at the time every twenty missions you had over the north, they applied a month of credit to your service requirement. I had flown about sixty something so I already had three months so they stopped me from flying until I finished my tour. But I still had 171 in the country and out of the country missions.

One of my roommates when I was in Vietnam was a guy named Guion Bluford. You might not know who he was but he was the first black man into space. He wasn't the first astronaut, but he was the first black man into space. As a matter of fact, I used to get on my soap opera box and tell all the guys, though there wasn't but a couple of us and say "Somebody has to be an astronaut." But when I had a chance to get out of the service, I went ahead and got out. Bluford told me later on, "You preached about being an astronaut, and you were the first one to cut out and go to the airlines." I told him "yeah, I had to do that because they were trying to bring me back over there again. I said, "I gave them enough chances to kill me; I'm not going to give them another chance."

It was very rewarding to see things that you wouldn't normally see. I remember during those days of Lyndon Johnson. I don't know whether you remember that Lyndon Johnson came to the base. I was there when he was there. I don't know how many bullet proof vests he had on, but he was standing up there and he was so stiff. He kind of looked like a stature. All of these guys were walking around with guns, m16's and all these kinds of things. Even though they are our own people, but still some people are crazy.

I've flown with an ex-president. What was the name of the man who used to hit his head all the time? He played football for Michigan. He was a very nice man. Secret Service guys would say, "You mind if I sit in First Class?" I'd say "Go ahead." Normally, they would ride in the cockpit just to make sure the pilot did what they were supposed to do.

They don't know anything about flying because if I'm flying captain and I got a copilot over there, I could turn the plane up side down before he could even do anything. You're better off in the air than you are on the ground. If you're brave enough to ride in a car on the road, you ought to be brave enough to get in an airplane because your chances of living are a lot better.

I've been asked if I could turn an airplane upside down. I said "yes, but you get all the fuel out of the wings and everything," I told Rev. Carter who's in my Sunday school class. He went to see the movie "Flight." He came back and said, you know, everything you told me was just right." I said, "Well I did fly them for about 40 years." It is possible to do this. You got to make sure that the wings do not have any fuel in them and make sure when you do the maneuver, you do it very gently in those kinds of conditions because you don't want to have too many negative gs on the wrong side of the wings. They sit downward not sitting upward and when you turn it over, now all the sets are not doing you any good because it's under the bottom, but it can be done.

I know you're a little bit older and I know you probably have grandsons and nieces and nephews. Sometimes you got to look at them and tell them that they are capable of doing anything. Don't let them think they can't or there's something they cannot do because they can do anything. My father only went to the 10th grade and has always taught me that you are no better than no one and no one is better than you. Try to learn something. Whatever you learn, they can't take it away from you.

I've had all kinds of ups and downs, some at my own hands even in schools I attended. I was supposed to be valedictorian of our class and they put a girl in front of me because her parents were teachers and my parents just worked in factories. But I'm just saying, you get adversity, you can get a bad teacher from anywhere. I was also taught, don't ever look at somebody and think they can't be your friend. When you get old, you can take your hands and you don't have but ten fingers if you're normal. But you're not going to get but ten really sho nuf good friends, so when one comes by, you keep him.

I flew with a guy, who was white. His name is Dick Mahler. He's a wonderful person, a wonderful person. This was years ago; he still calls me all the time. He lives in Seattle, Washington but he calls me all the time and every now and then he'll show up here in Georgia. He's just a wonderful human being. In this lifetime when you run into a good human being, a Christian person, nothing else matters. No matter how big he is, how tall he is, what color, all of that, it doesn't matter.

When I entered this building, I saw a lot of people talking with one another. I guess about things they did a while ago. Make sure that your grandkids know that they can do anything. I've got so many other experiences I would have to write them down. You don't want me to write all of the experiences, because some of them I don't want to remember.

But that's just the way it was, but I would always remember one thing, that God was always going to help me and when God has something for you, nobody on the face of this earth can walk around and call himself a man can stop you. It's impossible. Impossible because you can do anything you want to. You make sure they know this.

We were taught that we couldn't fly. It was said we couldn't be quarterback or center of a team. All of these things, and it wasn't true. Some of the best help we ever got was from other people. When "Chief" (Charles Alfred Anderson) learned how to fly, the one who was over the Tuskegee Airmen, he learned how to fly because he worked at the airport. He actually used to wash airplanes, taxi them around, getting them from one place to another and one man saw him doing this and said, "Um, I wonder if I can teach him how to fly"? He said it didn't take any time. The man came up, showed him how to fly and from that he got on with the Tuskegee Airmen. I don't know whether the man knew what he was doing. He wasn't a guy of our own color but he taught Chief how to fly and Chief taught all these guys how to fly, Benjamin Davis, Travis James and many more. He taught them all how to fly. So you just never know where your blessing is going to come from. Don't leave out anyone; take everybody for who they are and how they treat you.

Pinkney Mosley Jr. received a Bachelors Degree from Benedict College, and Masters Degree from the University of Utah. He served 6 years in the U. S. Air Force, and attained the rank of Captain. He flew 171 Missions in Viet Nam. He was a pilot for Delta Airlines for 33 years.

A Visit From Sweet Tyree and Friends

By
Richard D. Ashe

During the men's dormitory orientation session, the men's dormitory director, Mr. Joffery Whisenton, warned the guys that if a yearly pattern holds, some of the men would get a visit from a young man who calls himself "Sweet Tyree" who lived in the city. He said that Tyree usually made a visit during the first month of the school year and tries to befriend young men by offering expensive gifts.

Mr. Whisenton also indicated that in return for accepting Tyree's gifts, he expected something in return. At that point all the guys burst into laughter. No further details were given and no questions were asked. I basically dismissed such an encounter with Sweet Tyree as very remote.

Approximately a month later, I was sitting in my room studying when I heard a soft knock at the door. Upon opening the door, I saw three powered faced, curly headed, lip glossed, smiling young men. In a soft pitched voice the tallest one said, "Hi, my name is Sweet Tyree and these are my friends, Pookie, and Hammer. We were told that Richard Ashe lives on this floor." Feeling awkward and surprised, I said, "I'm Richard Ashe." Tyree then said, "May we come inside for a few minutes?" I nodded and said, "Sure." As the three entered they continued to smile and gaze at me. Not only did their visit puzzle me, but I wondered why I got a visit from these strange looking characters.

Their clothing was quite odd to me to the extent that I had never seen males dressed in tight shorts and flowery blouses. Tyree said, "We heard that you were quite an impressive looking guy. They were right." I said, "Thank you." He went on to say that they were here to make me an offer to become their friend. If I accepted I would be taken care of financially. Suddenly, Pookie's smile got wider then pulled the back bottom of his shorts and made an elastic pop. I surmised that he probably was wearing female under garments to get that sound.

Tyree then asked if I liked going to parties. I answered in the affirmative that I did. He said, "We are having a party Friday night. Would you like to attend?" Quickly, I said, "Sure, can I bring my girlfriend?" At that point all three visitors started laughing and saying, "He wants to bring his girlfriend!" The three headed towards the door. Tyree said, "I have a feeling that we are going to know each other very well."

Richard D. Ashe, Ph.D

After sharing my experience with my roommate, I dismissed it from my mind as an interesting encounter. Although Tyree's life style was very different from mine, I felt that everyone should always be treated with dignity and respect.

200

College Chaplain Gets Eyeful at Westminster House

By
Richard D. Ashe

The Westminster House was a multipurpose building utilized for small group sessions, prayer meetings and Sunday school classes. The building also housed the Office of the College Chaplain.

After eating dinner, tradition for several couples meant a regular stroll around the campus; time under the gigantic magnolia tree; a slow walk around the baseball field; sitting in the cement lawn chairs; or relaxing on the large entry ledges at Birthright auditorium. Some couples spent time studying together at the library.

One fall evening, the College Chaplain made his usual late evening visit to his office that was located in the rear of the multipurpose meeting area. Upon opening the door, the chaplain received an eyeful by observing a couple expressing their romantic affections for each other. The students were embarrassed and profusely expressed their sorrow and asked for forgiveness. The Chaplain accepted their apology and explained to the couple that he had an obligation to report the incident to the Dean's Office.

After the completion of a "due process hearing," the college suspended the students. The decision to suspend the students generated several days of argumentative discussions at the men's dormitory inside of John Know Hall.

Some argued that the administration was guilty of having an "entrapment policy for couples" by having an unlocked and unsupervised building. On the other hand, some argued that decisions by some students can be "over the top and way out of bounds."

Upon years of reflection on the incident at Westminster House, it seemed that it served as a kind of warning that mothers frequently give. "Always look before you leap."

Unofficial Card Parties at the Women's Dormitory

By

Richard D. Ashe

This author imagined that Willshoot, (not his real name) the security guard thought that he was in complete control and knowledgeable of the comings and goings of things after dark on Stillman's campus. But factually speaking, this was not the case at all. Willshoot would never have guessed how often he was outfoxed by students who decided to bend the rules.

Some male students knew his clocklike movements. They knew when he made his hourly rounds and how long it would take him to get from Point A to Point B. As a case in point, Chin, (not his real name) was a very popular figure on campus. Chin knew Willshoot's scheduled check points as well as Willshoot. Chin was very good at two other things...playing basketball and being an expert card player.

Richard D. Ashe, Ph.D

Every Saturday night at a designated arranged time, Chin and his favorite card playing pal would walk across the campus to check Willshoot's location. At an appropriate time Chin and his card playing buddy sprinted towards the thick shrubs at the bottom corner window at Geneva Hall, pecked on the window and immediately the window was raised by the female occupants of the room. An all night card playing party of bid whist and spades ensued until dawn. That's when Willshoot left campus for home.

Willshoot retired probably not knowing that for years, he had been outfoxed by a clever, popular and talented basketball player. Back then, the campus lighting was fair to dim. Now, the campus lighting is excellent. Security officials and monitors are strategically placed throughout the campus.

Santa Claus Ambushed Near Stillman College

(An Adult Holiday Story)
By
Richard D. Ashe

(The following story is meant to tease my friend, Robert Burns about his hobby of deer hunting. In no way is this story intended to disparage the good character of loyal supporters of Stillman College.)

One New Year's Eve, Santa Claus and his usual reindeer crew were flying high in the sky to celebrate the coming of a new year. On the celebration tour with Santa was: Dasher, Dancer, Prancer, Vixen, Comet, Cupid, Blitzen and Rudolf. Also hitched to Santa's sleigh were three new reindeers that Santa was training to deliver toys to children during Christmas.

While Santa and the reindeer glided over the blue darkening skies of Alabama, Santa decided to find a suitable farm field for the deer to eat before heading back to the North Pole. In the meantime, Robert Burns was hosting an annual deer hunting party at his farm located several miles near Stillman College. The hunters were waiting to see if deer in the nearby forest would come and provide them with sufficient gourmet meals for the remainder of the winter. With riffles in arms, the hunters, Peter Millet, Bruce Crawford, Robert Burns, Alfonso Gooden, Frederick Blackburn, Tommy Woods, Hayward Strickland, Robert Heath, George Rutherford, Floyd Phillips and Anthony Holloman were eagerly waiting and ready for action.

From above in the evening sky, Santa spotted several bales of hay and a creek on a farm. Santa thought this was an ideal place for the deer to eat and get fresh water before proceeding for home. Santa and his reindeer landed at the Robert Burns Farm. As the deer were eating, the hunters raised their rifles and fired. Santa, seeing his new deer lying mortally wounded, shouted for the other deer to retreat to the sleigh for an emergency take off. Safely in the sky, Santa and his deer had mixed feelings of emotions. They were sad that they had lost three deer friends. They were also happy that the rest of the crew were safe and heading home. On the other hand, the hunters at the Robert Burns Farm were jubilant. The remains of three deer would provide delicious meat for their friends and families throughout the winter. All of the hunters danced, sang, and shouted out with merriment and lots of glee.

Incident At Mom's Party House

By
Richaard D. Ashe

One Weekend a couple of fellow dormitory students and I decided to treat ourselves to an hour or two of relaxation at Mom's Party House. Mom's Party House was the very place that our dormitory director, Joffre Whisenton had warned us about going there during our orientation. He said that he felt uncomfortable with students going there due to the place's reputation. In spite of the dormitory director's apprehension, this was a regular hangout for several students during the weekend.

Students who were familiar with Mom's Party House indicated that visitors had an option of playing cards, dancing or listening to records. Then, there was the opportunity to buy a bottle of beer or a shot of whisky. Mom, the home owner could be described as chubby but friendly and she wore red lipstick. She would greet her customers with a friendly smile and hello. She was also the barmaid. Students who frequently visited Mom's Party House also informed us that there was a "good looking house entertainer." Her name was Millie.

As we entered the party house we observed that there were three other customers there, a couple and young man. The couple was dancing and the young man who was very muscular looked to be in his early 20's stood against the wall. After the three of us had been at Mom's Party House for approximately thirty minutes, each Stillmanite was enjoying the music and observing the couple dance. When Mom played the upbeat song called "Work with me Annie," Millie the house entertainer asked me to dance with her. I obliged. The two of us did the "swing dance" which was quite prevalent among young people during that time.

The two of us were swinging wide and enjoying the music as well as the chemistry of each others dance movements. While dancing and at the point when my back was directly in front of the muscular young man standing against the wall, he stepped forward and pushed me in my back rather forcibly. This unexpected two hand push to my back not only startled me but almost made me fall. Immediately, the young man and I met in the center of the room. Needless to say, I was furious at this unwarranted attack upon my body. I was ready to retaliate rather forcefully.

I was joined by my Stillman friends who were with me. At that moment I had to make a choice. Do I follow the advice that I had received early in my childhood and neighborhood friends which was, "If someone put their hands on you, retaliate with all your might." Another choice for me was to allow someone that I didn't know determine my future. My two friends and I could have handled this guy and put a big hurting on him. My thinking at the time was, if we choose this route, we could end up paying a heavy price. We came to Stillman to get an education, not go to jail or prison.

Mom, the owner of Mom's House Party had observed what had happened, and said to my two Stillman friends and me, "Let it go!" Don't jeopardize your future! Although her advice was hard to swallow, I realized that her advice was excellent and the best choice for us to make. My friends and I returned to Stillman's campus and never returned to Mom's Party House again.

Over the years as a school administrator, I counseled many students who felt that they were disrespected by other individuals. My advice to them was to consider a quotation of mine which says, **"It's not so much about the disrespect that you receive, but how you choose to respond to the disrespect."**

Embarrassing Moments or Devine Intervention?

By
Richard D. Ashe

For whatever reason, there are times when embarrassing experiences happen to all of us at unexpected times and places. Consequently, I was on the receiving end of such an occasion. My experience reminded me when Dr. Franklin, a History professor at Stillman was the featured speaker at chapel service. Dr. Franklin stumbled and almost fell as he approached the podium. The tough and rigid professor's unexpected moment caused me to chuckle. Needless to say, I was admonished by upper classmen.

First of all, I should preface my unexpected experience by stating that mentally, I have held a distained opinion of individuals whose cell phone would ring in meetings or places where silence was expected and appropriate.

Recently at the funeral of a fellow church member at Elizabeth Baptist Church, (Atlanta) I approached the microphone to read a Ministry Resolution to salute the outstanding service career of the deceased. Suddenly and very loudly my new phone that I had just purchased and was unfamiliar with its features began to ring. Stunned and very embarrassed, I frantically attempted to shut the phone off with little success. I squeezed, pushed and shook the phone hoping that somehow the phone would stop ringing.

In the meantime, I apologized to Pastor Craig Oliver, the grieving family and even to the deceased that lay in the casket. While attempting to silence the phone, Pastor Oliver, the grieving family members and funeral attendees in the church were laughing hardily at my awkward and frantic efforts to turn the phone off.

Finally, after succeeding to place the phone in silent mode, I said to the funeral attendees that the deceased would have liked being saluted by a telephone. After reading the Ministry Resolution, I asked everyone to give the deceased an ovation as a tribute to her life long service to the church. The entire audience responded by standing with a loud and prolonged applause.

As for me, I no longer will look down mentally at anyone for forgetting to place their phone on "silent mode." After all, all of us make mental mistakes. The Ministry President, Sharon Sterling told me that I "changed a solemn home going service to a home going celebration." Now when I go to church, I get lots of smiles, while several church members refer to me as "The Telephone Man."

Children Deserve A Chance At Safe Life

By
Richard D. Ashe

The current social events of today remind me of the lively discussions that we had in my social studies classes as a student at Stillman College. Some of the issues discussed and debated were voting rights; crime; high unemployment numbers for minority youth; the staggering number of youth being sent to prison for an extensive period of time; and the hot button issue of gun ownership and violence.

After the recent shootings at Sandy Hook Elementary School, Columbine and Heritage High Schools many were asking the question, "Why?" The question that could have been asked is, "What can we do to give our children a better chance at life and safety?"

The truth of the matter is that the violence that we read about and see during the morning and evening television news did not just begin to happen overnight. It began decades ago. As we grew as a nation, little by little the violence grew as well.

At times when I read about the senseless killings and shootings, I can't help but to wish that those distinguished men of wisdom who wrote the United States Constitution would have rephrased a small portion of that great document which speaks of our right to bear arms.

It would be foolish to blame entirely our right to bear arms for the never-ending drum beat of murders that take place in our country. We must also look at the public's love of macho men displaying their exotic and sophisticated weapons of destruction in movies and video games.

Our violent times can also be attributed to the deterioration of our family structure. For many years the family was the cohesive fabric that held us together as a community and as a people. Somehow we must find a way to restore this important entity.

Finger-pointing and assigning blame for what is happening to our youth could be done, but what purpose would it serve? The thing that we need to do is to ask ourselves the question, "When are we, the people, going to decide that corrective action is urgently needed?"

When we decide that a bold and collective plan of action and involvement is needed to stop this madness of violence, educators, religious, community and political leaders will be saying loud and clear that our children deserve a better chance at life and safety.

THE SPIRITUAL FRONT

"Food, clothing and shelter bind us to a common bond,
but mutual respect is required before
going to the great beyond."

R. D. Ashe

CHAPTER SIX

The Spiritual Front

A Family Morning Prayer

By
Michelle A. Ross

Our Father, we thank You for another day and for allowing us to wake up once again in our right mind. We thank You for watching over us as we slept during the night. We invite Your presence to be among us this morning to give Your assurance of Your love and compassion for each of us.

This morning, we bow in worship and praise before You. We come to You in prayer because when we pray to You, we are spending time in Your presence. In prayer, we find physical and spiritual comfort that this family needs and desires.

Dear God, this is a new day and we may face unexpected temptations. Please help us to keep free from evil and detrimental choices. When we meet others may they see You in our words and deeds. We pray that You lift everything that concerns us this morning and ask that You work it out for the greater good to glorify Your righteous and Holy name.

We realize that in everyone's life, we travel through mountains of pain and suffering. Allow our trials and tribulations to be a testimony of how You put Your arms around us simply because we believe in You and that You will be with us in every conflict, storm and life situation. We believe that You may allow suffering and challenges come into our lives and the lives of loved ones to make us more appreciative, kinder and helpful. But most of all we feel that You allow challenges to come into our lives to make us stronger and wiser.

Dear Lord, You know that we are mortals and capable of evil and sin. We ask You to forgive us of our sins and transgressions. Help us to forgive those who trespass against us as You have forgiven us of our sins through word, thought and deed.

As we conclude our family prayer session this morning, we pray that You bless our home, loved ones and our needs. We pray that You bless our schools, places of worship and our youth. We ask that You guide us, protect us, and be gracious and merciful to us.

These and other blessings we ask in Your Holy name. Amen, Amen, and Amen.

Michelle A. Ross is a 1991 graduate from Stillman College. She received her MA degree from Clark Atlanta University and her Ed.S from Lincoln Memorial University.

Our Spiritual Creed

(A Responsive Reading)

Leader:

Allow the trumpets to sound and let the drums thunder to mighty beats.
Let the bells toll for our ancestral souls to be at peace and ease.

All:

Our destiny is in our hands for opportunities to seize.
Let us work, study, pray and sing 'til justice is completely blind
And righteous is truly intertwined.

Leader:

We incline our hearts and ears to His will,
May He grant His mercy and spirit to guide us along the way;
While avoiding temptations that would have us sway.

All:

**We travel paths that's stained with bitter fears, tears and pain,
Yet, we gladly honor Him for sunshine and the challenges He
brings.**

Leader:

Letting our steps be guided by what is true and what is right,
We'll be guided by His light.

All:

**If injustice rears its monstrous head, let it be said, we chose to
fight with The Master's armor instead.**

Leader:

We acknowledge that our God is the stronghold of our lives,
We glorify the beauty of His works on land, at sea and in the sky.

All:

Blessed to have the power and courage to soar,
We lift our praises to Him, who is worthy to be praised for
evermore.

Richard D. Ashe

Take Time to Savor the Relationship of the Magnolia

By
Reverend Isaiah Sumbry

The Bible speaks of various relationships that one can discover. Therefore, as we think about the goodness of what God has done in all of our lives even as we have or currently matriculating throughout the grounds of our beloved Stillman College, let us pause to reflect on our relationships. As we think about the significance of relationships, a well remembered religious mandated study guide was introduced to me as I was adopted into the family of Stillmanites was "The Book." The Book is better known by many through the ages as "<u>The Holy Bible</u>." The Book reminded me of the need for spiritual as well as a loving and neighboring relationship.

Stillman has always been an institution of higher learning where relationships are constantly being formed. As you begin to look up at your developing relationships, realize that some will be short-lived while others will be life-long. Moreover, during our educational development we find that these relationships have challenged us to mature spiritually and socially. Therefore, as we equip our minds and cultivate our talents in order to be able to facilitate and serve the greater good of mankind, we must remain focused at all times because this moment of opportunity is not a recurring event.

So, if you find yourself walking under the magnolia trees and the leaves are beginning to fall or the blooms are commencing to break forth, notice that it's just a reminder that seasons do appear in all our lives. The sweet aroma that is incensed in our minds is a reminder that one day all of our days of matriculating from financial halls, educational halls, dining and student centers, and athletic facilities will end. However, the relationships with faculty, staff, and fellow students will be etched in the bark of our own individual magnolia tree.

I have always found amazement in where life leads after the years of collegiate preparation. I knew what I wanted to be, but for some reason there has always been another divinely plan for our lives. So as you continue to feel the wind blowing through the branches of the magnolias, and hear the sound of chimes making melodious music far above the warrior water, let us continue to raise our hymn to thee, recognizing that we really don't know about tomorrow. We just live from day to day. We don't borrow from its sunshine for its clouds may turn to gray. We don't even worry over the future for we know what Jesus said, "I'll never leave you nor forsake you." Today, I'll walk beside Him, for He knows what lies ahead.

Reverend Isaiah Sumbry received his BA degree from Stillman College in 1984.

Pulling Down of Strongholds

11 Corinthians 10:3-5

By

Vernon Swift

"Pulling Down of Strongholds" is part of a collection of my sermons and lectures featured in **Hiding Behind The Blood.** I am honored to submit this sermon to be included in the Inspirational Chapter of this book, **Under the Magnolia Tree.**

The strongholds that I am going to speak on are not physical; not fleshly, but they are spiritual. It is a spiritual battle. You can be in spiritual bondage, walking around in prison spiritually.

Let me tell you what a stronghold is. A stronghold is a forceful, stubborn argument of rationale or opinion or ideal or philosophy that is formed; it can form itself in your mind. And it is resistant to the knowledge of Jesus Christ. Let me say that again. Opinion, ideal, rationale, philosophy, stubborn argument—you can have some stubborn arguments and thoughts in your mind. Those are strongholds because as a man thinketh in his heart, so is he. It starts with your thought process. In fact, everything you do starts with a thought and moves to attitude. That attitude becomes an action which can form a habit or an addiction. But it starts with your thinking. That is why Paul said, … "but we have the mind of Christ." That is why he said to the Romans that we ought to have a renewed mind. A person's mind can be entangled. Let me tell you how entangled. You can be so entangled that if you feel in your mind that you cannot do something, you will not do it. That is why you should not tell that child: "Boy your grandfather wasn't anything, your daddy wasn't anything, and you are not anything either." I do not care what they were; you can be somebody because you are somebody. You are hearing this message is significant to God. The fact that God woke you up this morning denotes that God is not finished with you yet. Now, you need to find out what God wants you to do. Ask Him because you are somebody with God. You think He will continue to let your heart beat and continue giving you fresh air, oxygen and then just let you continue your contrary ways? No, you are somebody to God. And you should tell yourself, "I am a child of God."

Our children are getting back to school. We have had a banquet for them, a program for them. We gave school supplies and our prayers. We have been pushing them to be successful to let them know they can make it. Do not let them go to school thinking that they cannot make it. Tell these students that they can make all A's and that they need to do the best they can. Students, you are not square if you are in a class where you make all A's. It is a great class to be in. You should tell them that they can be successful. They have that exit exam, but if our children start passing it with flying colors, they will move that exit exam out of the school system. That is just a stronghold. We have so many strongholds to hold our people back to let them feel that they cannot make it. Everyone can make it. You have the same brain. God has given you knowledge, the Lord is with you. You can make it. You do not have to be in a class with somebody that has a different color than you have to make it. If God is with you, you can make it by yourself. Somebody knows what I am talking about. Reason. I know you can. I grew up in times when we got the leftover schoolbooks and leftover desks. But, that did not embarrass me. We walked to school. When we received books, those other folk names were already in the books. The other folks had a manual edition of the book; they had a newer book, and we had the old books, but guess what? We made it. When we got home, our parents told us to get our lessons out and study. When we came to the table, we all came together, and everybody said their Bible verse. They let us know that it was God who was providing for us. We need to teach our children this same fact.

We need to gather at home—pray at home. Nobody can take prayer from anybody. You cannot take prayer out of school. We let these folks rock us to sleep, talking about "Supreme Court has taken prayer out of the schools, child, what are you going to do about that." I am not worried about that because wherever a child of God is he can pray.

That Phoenician woman in the 15th Chapter of Matthew just said, "Lord, help me. My daughter is grievously vexed with a devil but help me Lord." And guess what? Jesus saw her faith. If you have faith to pray, you do not have to open your mouth to pray, just say "Lord have mercy upon my child." God can destroy yokes. Let me tell you. The answer is right here. The answer is you. You have a praying place.

Strongholds are demonic. They are not from God. Anything that opposes Christ and is against Jesus is of the devil. Jesus said, "If you are not for me, you are against me." I have been in church meetings when I see some people will not vote either way. That is a vote against. "Child, I am just not going to have anything to do with it." You are either for the proposed idea or you are against it. That is a dangerous person. Let me tell you. If you have a friend who will not speak up for you when you need him to speak up, that friend is worse than your worst enemy. That is not your friend. That is worse than the one who is against you.

Strongholds. They are demonic. Look at what it says. "The weapons of our warfare are not carnal," which means they are not fleshly, "but they are mighty through God." You have some might; you have the mighty power of God to the pulling down strongholds. Look what these strongholds are in verse 5: "casting down imaginations." Let me tell you that Satan can let you just sit in here and imagine every bad thing about everybody. Look at the good. Everybody has some good. They put their clothes on this morning. That is good, is it not? Imagination. "And every high thing that exalted itself against the knowledge of God." And then God gives you the power to bring into captivity every thought. We need to capture the thought and make our thoughts obedient to Christ.

Let us look at some types of strongholds. I told you that they are demonic. Fear is a stronghold. Some people are just fearful. They are fearful to venture out. You know the opposite of fear is faith. Faith gets God excited. Did you know that God is excited with you? Just take Him at His word. I am going to do it because God says do it. Satan wants you to stay in fear. I cannot do this; I cannot do that. I am fearful. My mommy had cancer; my daddy had cancer; Lord I hope I do not. You just keep on. You do not have what somebody else had. Do not live in fear. You say what God says, I am healed, because God says I am healed. I am healed because by His stripes I am healed. I am healed because He wants me to prosper and be in health even as my soul prospers. Fear. Some people have fear of being rejected. Some people have fear of being lonely. I had a young lady say, "I've got to find me a husband, I'm getting older. I don't want to live my life in loneliness." If you have Jesus, you do not have to be lonely. Some ladies have husbands, have been married a long time, and they are still lonely. Some husbands walk around opening car doors for the woman, and when she is at home, she is still lonely. Do not get mad with me let me tell you. Live your life in the word of God.

Anna was a prophetess, but do you know what she did? She stayed in the temple and she was happy praising God with prayer and fasting. And do you know what happened one day while she was doing that? Mary and Joseph walked in. Mary had Jesus in her arms. Let me tell you. If you stay with the Lord, He will show up. And when He shows up, you can have some joy and never be alone. You have somebody with you. So many of us live our lives in loneliness and emptiness.

The word admonishes what we say to God. Get you a song and make melody in your heart. Do you know what a friend you have in Jesus? He bears all our sins and grief. What a privilege it is to carry everything to God in prayer. God can remove that loneliness and emptiness. Some people want a bigger house. Let me tell you that if you are not happy where you are, a bigger house just gives you more rooms in which to be miserable. If you have Jesus, and you are satisfied with a shotgun house you can go to sleep at night, and you do not have to take a sleeping pill. You are in good hands. When God promotes, then you can go on and be happy. Some people are fearful of the future. They worry about what is going to happen tomorrow.

Let me tell you something. You should learn from experiences. Jesus fed five thousand men, not counting women and children, with two fish and five loaves, and later on, the multitude got hungry again and became fearful. Jesus said, "Why are you fearful. Don't you remember how I fed five thousand? And I said that to say this, the same God I know from past experiences is the God who brought me thus far. Many may try to destroy you, but God can make good out of it. Satan meant it for your failure, but God made good out of it.

Joseph's brothers sold him because they envied and hated him. They sold him, but read the footnote; wherever Joseph was the Bible said, "God was with him." I do not care where you are. If god is with you, you can make it. Do not go around talking about, "I don't have anybody; my folks don't like me; mommy don't like me." No, pull down that stronghold. We have Jesus; we can make it. Potiphar gave Joseph control of everything in his household except his wife. Then when his wife made a pass at him, Joseph left the house running. Potiphar's wife lied about him. Potiphar put him in prison. But guess what? God was with him. Let me tell you that when God is with you, you can make it. I do not care who is against you. If god is for you, He is more than the world against you. Pull down that stronghold. Joseph was in charge even in prison. He went from a prisoner to president. When they needed a secretary of agriculture, they tried to find somebody who possessed the spirit of the Lord. And they looked at Joseph and said, "You're the man." And Joseph ended up being in charge of all the agriculture in Egypt. Now, the ones who sold him were the ones in trouble. They said, "When daddy dies Joseph is going to get back after us. He's going to retaliate." Joseph said, "O, No! You meant it for evil but God made good out of it."

Look at Jesus. They nailed Him to an old rugged cross. They put a thorny crown on His head and mocked Him. They derided and beat Him. They brought false accusations against Him, but Jesus would not jump down from the cross and beat everybody up. Jesus would not say, "Go on and beat me up; you just wait until Sunday morning, I will get up and get you back." He hung right there and said, "Father, forgive them; for they know not what they do." Please remember if you stay with the Lord, you can pull down the strongholds.

Another stronghold is anger. Some people are just mad, are they not? They are just angry. They are angry about something somebody has done to them. Listen, that is not your problem; that is the problem of folks who put themselves in that position. Let people do whatever they want to do you. Let them say whatever they want to say about you. You just go down in prayer. Let me tell you what you should do with your anger. First of all, do not nurse your anger. It will eat at your soul and destroy your life. People live in houses with each other angry; just angry. Do not nurse it.

Secondly, do not rehearse your anger. Do not go around telling everybody else about it. I am mad with so and so. Some people go all over town being mad with you, and they want everybody else in town to be mad with you. Some folks do not like you and they want everybody else not to like you. Some folks will do that. Do not rehearse your anger. That is a stronghold. That thing will have you so tangled up until you cannot go to sleep at night. That person who got you angry is somewhere sleeping, and you are somewhere trying to take a pill to go to sleep. You are somewhere with high blood pressure; you are somewhere with a heart attack. The person who got you all messed up is going on his way. Do not rehearse your anger.

Thirdly, do not disperse it. Do not fight back. But I will tell you what to do, reverse it. Do you know how to reverse your anger? Well, Ephesians 4:31, 32 tell you how to reverse your anger. It says, "Let all bitterness, and wrath, and anger, and clamor, and evil speaking, be put away from you, ... and be ye kind one to another." Yes, that is how you reverse anger. Be kind to one another. Well, you might say, "I do not feel good about it." Well, Jesus did not feel good either. He did not feel good about being beaten all night, but thank God, they buried Him. But God raised Him. If you do what Jesus did, God can fight your battle. Somebody knows He is a battle-ax in the time of war. Be tenderhearted, forgiving one another, even as God for Christ's sake has forgiven you. I just want to tell you to stay with the Lord. Get the work of God in your heart. Do not be angry with anybody. It will eat at your soul.

Another stronghold is a cutting tongue. I know some people say, "this is my tongue; I will do what I want to do with it," I say what I want to say with it." But Proverbs 15:1 says, ... "grievous words stir up anger," and Proverbs 12:18 says, ... "the tongue of the wise is health." Whatever you say to someone, if it is not going to edify them, you should not say it because words are important. You should speak health to one another.

The last stronghold I want to discuss is low self-esteem. I have already told you that you are somebody. We should tell children that they can be successful because they are somebody. The folks on the other side of town do not control who I am. I am a child of God. Putting a certain uniform on does not describe who I am. I am a child of God. You have been washed in the blood of the Lamb; you have been born of the Spirit of God. God has given you some power. The power is within you. I know the power is within you because Ephesians 3:20 says, "Now unto Him who is able to do exceeding abundantly above all that we ask or think," but it is "according to the power that worketh in us."

Thank God, we have some power; the power is a mighty power pulling down strongholds. I am so glad that Satan cannot handle us. You see the reason that I know he cannot handle us is that Jesus fought the battle at Calvary. Satan shot his best shot on a hill called Calvary. He thought he was working against Jesus, but he was working right into God's hand. Do you not hear Isaiah saying, "He was wounded for our transgressions, He was bruised for our iniquities: the chastisement of our peace was upon Him; and with His stripes we are healed." Let his mind be in you that was also in Christ Jesus." When that mind is in you, you can say, "I have what God says I have; I am what God says I am; I can do what God says I can do. I am healed because God says I am healed. I am rich because God says I am rich." Then when you pull down the strongholds you should praise the Lord. "This is my story, this is my song praising my Savior all the day long." I am praising my Savior all the day long.

Rev. Vernon Swift received an Associate of Arts degree from Mary Holmes College, the BA degree from Stillman College, and the Master's degree from the University of Alabama.

The Shiloh United Methodist Church

Sermon# 060312

Scripture: Hebrews 9:15

Sermon Title

"Love and Happiness"

By
Rev. Dr. Wayne D. Mims

<Scripture>

1 John 4:7-10

Dear friends, let us love one another, for love comes from God. Everyone who loves has been born of God and knows God. Whoever does not love does not know God, because God is love. This is how God showed his love among us: He sent his one and only Son into the world that we might live through him. This is love: not that we loved God, but that he loved us and sent his Son as an atoning sacrifice for our sins.

"Love and Happiness"

I am reminded of a song by the Rev. Al Green, *"Love and Happiness"* in which it encompasses a multitude of things that we grapple with on a daily basis and if you do not mine I would like to explore the song for just a moment. It says, *love and happiness ... something that can make you do wrong, make you do right.* People all over the world are searching for love and happiness, yet few find it. So you may begin to ask yourself the question why? The answer is that few people know what LOVE is and still fewer know how it can be attained. See, when we desire something we know what it is that we want and if we have a strong enough desire for it we discover the means of acquiring it, but love and happiness that which people desire above all else they find the greatest difficulty in achieving. We pursue it in a thousand ways and the more furious our pursuit, the more it eludes them. The truth is, as long as people set happiness before them as a goal, whether in the appearance of wealth, fame or security, they will not attain it. Love and happiness has nothing to do with objects or places, space or time. People often think: "If I only had a house of my own I would be happy." Or, "If only I earned double my salary I would be happy." Or "If I could live in this place or that place I would be happy." The attainment of such objectives cannot bring happiness. It may bring momentary pleasure or delight, but they do not lead to lasting satisfaction of love and happiness. It is not the place nor the condition but the state of mind alone that can make anyone happy or miserable. It is time for us to recognize that love and happiness does not come from things but from God.

Now, I would like to extrapolate, pontificate and coagulate the chosen periscope. The Bible tells us that we are to establish a relationship with God. When we are in the process of developing the fullness and intimacy of our relationship with a God of love, and maintaining that participation of nature in which love is of God, and he who loves is born of God partakes therefore of His nature, and knows Him for it is by faith that he received it as partaking of His nature. He who loves not does not know God. We must possess the nature that loves in order to know what love is. He then who does not love does not know God, for God is LOVE. Such a person has not one sentiment in connection with the nature of God; how then can he know Him? No more than an animal can know what a man's mind or understanding is when he has not got it. The eternal life which was with the Father has been manifested and has been imparted to us thus we are partakers of the divine nature. The affections of that nature acting in us rest, by the power of the Holy Spirit, in the enjoyment of communion with God who is its source; we dwell in him and him in us. The acting of this nature proves that He dwells, if we love, God Himself dwells in us. He who works this love is there but He is infinite and the heart rests in Him; we know at the same time that we dwell in Him, and He in us, because He has given us of His Spirit but this passage, so rich in blessing, demands that we should follow it with order. For you see love makes everything alright. When you allow yourself to love you receive the benefits of being loved back. When you allow yourself to go there in love you will see mountains moved. You will see life changing experiences. You will feel like you never have before. For you see, you must be willing to love with your whole heart. You must be willing to give all of you in order to receive all the love that God has for you. You must understand that love is a state of being, not an emotion, not a choice; for it is an ability. When we are ready to give love, receive love, and endure love; it will become a present force in our lives so if you are ready to have a little love in your life you must allow God to penetrate your heart and give Him all of you because when you are in right relationship with God you will attain true love and happiness.

Love and happiness is not just a feeling or emotion but it is thirsting for a connection with God, therefore; I want to give you 3 things to help us have love and happiness.

1st of all we must want to be happy. Everybody wants to <u>achieve happiness</u>, but how many of us are truly happy. Do you know why happiness is so elusive to most of us? Aristotle once said, "Happiness is the meaning and the purpose of life, the whole aim and end of human existence." Our sole purpose in life is nothing but achieving happiness. We do everything in life to find happiness. We look for it in love, owning a beautiful house, having a satisfying and well-paid job, getting married, staying healthy, spending time with loved ones, achieving your dreams, be liked and loved. Ironically, the search for happiness is one of the chief sources of unhappiness. Some say happiness is a state of mind. The very source of true happiness lies in our mind, and not in external circumstances. See if we truly want to be happy we can change our external circumstances in order to achieve this goal. How you view yourself and your world are our conscious choices. We choose not to be happy ... Staying in bad relationships ... Staying at a dead end job ....Your thoughts determines and interprets what is happening around you but you can choose to find happiness in small, everyday things. You can choose to interpret what happens in a positive way or in a negative way and your choices control much of how much happiness you will find and create in your life. So you see, our actions and conditions dictate if we truly want to be happy.

2ndly to achieve happiness we must overcome negativity and count our blessings. You need to let go and release the need to control. One key way to achieve happiness is letting go, forgive and move on. Let go of anger, jealousy, dejection, or pride but the truth is you have a choice to decide not to be angry, depressed or dejected. You know that all these negative and energy sapping thoughts do more harm than good. Instead we should find a way how to get rid of these past useless thoughts as they are hindering our path to happiness. Stop holding on to attachment to old stuff that we know is holding us back. We must remember life goes on. It is possible to live happily-ever-after on a day-to-day basis making the most of every opportunity to love those whom we care for and be happy. Our life is defined by moment by moment in the present, as long as our heart keeps beating. If you are not truly happy today it is time for you to step out on faith and gain yourself a piece of love and happiness. Remember, the past is over and the future is yet to come. All you have is the present and it is happening right now. Yesterday is history.

Tomorrow is a mystery and today is a gift. That's why we call it the present. We do not have control over time, but we can consciously live life fully and happily in the present moment. To live in the present moment requires awareness and deliberate effort to focus our minds on what we are doing or experiencing now. Negativity prevents us from receiving all of the love and happiness that God has ordained for your life.

3rdly our happiness lies with Jesus. The wisdom of our world tells us that happiness comes with success or pre-eminence in our chosen field, with wealth whether through enterprise or the Lottery, or with celebrity status, even the fleeting status of TV fame. Happiness, we are told, comes from the way in which we are regarded by society. "Yet, in our hearts, we know this is not so, even while being tempted to follow such siren voices. We know that our happiness lies much closer to home in our steady relationships of friendship and love in family and community. But you must understand that we all can find true happiness and that is in Jesus the Christ. He is at the heart of this revelation, at the heart of happiness, for in his every word and action he will disclose the truth, not only of God but also of our own humanity. He is the one at the centre of our joy. For you see, only when we grasp that Jesus is truly God and truly man that we will fill the gulf between us and God. Our growth and contentment lies in being faithful to Jesus. We must always give thanks for what you have. Focus on your blessings and not what you don't have in your life. If there is something that you want; go get it but appreciate the little things in life. See, we should thank God for waking us up each morning, for food on your table, for family and friends. Pray every day that you will remain blessed. For you see, if you really want true love and happiness I recommend a lover to you. He may not wear the finest clothes but he has on pure white robe. He might not be the tallest man in the world but he has the weight of the world on his shoulders. He might not have a Lexis or BMW or a 5000ft house at Eagles Landing but he has prepared a place for you in heaven. That place of refuge in Heaven you will have Jesus the one who sticks closer than a brother, the one who will make a way out of no way, your balm in Gilead, your wheel in the middle of a wheel for he is the lily of the valley and the bright and morning star. Love and happiness may not come from things but we must focus on grace, not goodness. We must focus on God's work, not worth. When we focus on God we will attain love and happiness.

Wayne D. Mims obtained degrees from the following institutions:

Bachelor of Arts degree – Stillman College
Master of Divinity—Interdenominational Theological Center [Gammon Theological Seminary]
Doctor of Ministry—Northwestern Theological Seminary

Spiritulosophy

By
C. J. Johnson

(C. J. Johnson's extraordinary personal experiences in college and the workforce intertwine for exceptional reading and enjoyment. The author of **Under the Magnolia Tree** has taken the liberty to proclaim him to be an "Honorary Stillmanite." and included five excerpts of his Seven Tenants of **Spiritulosophy:** A New Approach to Old Truths.)

I.   ACCEPT THAT THERE IS A GOD

(Or "Higher Power," "Creator," "Divine Presence" Or Just Bigger Than Yourself)

If you look at the moon, the stars, the night, the day, and the changing of the seasons, you know that there is some being or some force that has put these things in motion. Even some atheists (who say God does not exist) and some agnostics (who say there is no way to prove one way or another) believe in what scientist call "intelligent design." When you look at a Scarlet Macaw—that's that big, pretty parrot-like bird that has brilliant colors of blue, red, yellow, green and purple that are so brilliant that artists can't duplicate the colors exactly, or a zebra whose striped patterns are unique from every other zebra, yet symmetric so that if you draw a line down the middle it looks and measures the exact same on both sides—you know there's divine order from a creator who is perhaps just "showing off."

Just accept, though, that we (humans) simply can't understand how creation was carried out because we aren't capable. There is some "thing" bigger and more powerful intelligent-wise than we are!! There is force that exists in a higher realm than we can reach or even see; we can vaguely imagine. Besides, who gave man the intellectual capacity and ingenuity for all the technology (some which has been misused) that he has developed? Why does a sexual orgasm feel good? Why do our favorite foods and beverages taste good? Who gave us these senses? Perhaps the mere fact that we can even conceive of God and question his existence means that he (or she) has to exist. Surely, such enormous of a Supreme Being couldn't have possibly entered into our imagination unless that Supreme Being put it there.

To illustrate, as far as recorded history goes back, history indicates that man has always pondered the existence of many gods in general or one main God in particular.

II.   DON'T BE AFRAID TO "ASK"

Very often in our daily lives, we are given information. This information comes from the work place, from the media, from our social activities, etc. Much of the information doesn't really matter because, although it may impact us somewhat, often there's not a whole lot we can do to change it. In other words, we simply accept the information without much investigation of its validity. But when it comes to matters of the heart, soul, or mind, such as information that relates to religion, the information must be thoroughly investigated because our reliance on this information shapes our lives, our children's lives, and possibly the lives of those close to us.

Even though it may be convenient to accept what the pastor or spiritual leaders' concept of how to govern our lives is—especially if it is in line with what we've believed all our lives or what our parents, guardians, or significant others have taught us ("It was good for my dear mother, it's good enough for me!") we shouldn't be reluctant to get clarification, or even verification if we don't feel completely comfortable with the information we've been given. That's why I ASK (Always Seek Knowledge) about matters of importance in general, and about religion in particular. After "ASKing," I've discovered that facts that my pastors, teachers or professors, and even parents never taught me or exposed to me.

III. DON'T BE AFRAID TO THINK OUTSIDE THE BOX

For all of our lives, in one way or another, in one setting or another, there have been standardized rules, policies or etiquette that dictate how we should behave ourselves in certain situations. These rules, policies and etiquette range from laws that govern the overall well being of society (The 10 Commandments, criminal and civil laws, etc), to proper manners ("Yes Ma'am," "Please," "Thank You," "Excuse Me,"etc., to what to wear at a formal affair and what fork to use when eating at a dinner, as well as other expectations of social behavior. In fact, all of these rules, policies, and etiquette can form a type of "box" that people are expected to stay in, and, also, for the most part, the staying inside this box by everyone serves as an advantage for the peace and harmony of the public and, most importantly, the avoidance of anarchy.

But folks, I urge you: Do keep everything you do in its proper perspective, but don't be fundamental about your views. You see folks, in addition to a box that covers how we should govern ourselves socially—not surprisingly, but unfortunately—there sometimes exists another "box covering how we should think and even—in some cases—how we should feel." At this point I ask a question: As long as what you do or think is not intended to hurt someone or interfere with what someone does (as long as they aren't being harmful to others), why should you deny your freedom by thinking "outside the box"?

Be aware though, because in order to not be afraid to think outside the box, there are a couple of bold things you must do:

A. Have the Courage to be Different. Let me give you a true story that exemplifies this concept.

Once, while I was working at a small Law Firm, the company had exceeded its quarterly goals, reaching productivity levels never before accomplished, thereby setting a company record. To reward the employees, the owners-partners of the firm decided to take the employees and their one guest out to celebrate with dinner and drinks. For organizational purpose, they requested that the employees fill out a list consisting of who would be attending, whether or not they would bring a guest, and their choice of the restaurant they desired. This was necessary - the owners said - because they wanted to have some idea of how many people were expected to attend so the venue of our choice could make proper accommodations and for budgeting purposes as well.

On the day that the list was generated and distributed, for some reason, I arrived to work late. Someone as I recall: my manager advised me that if I wanted to attend the celebration, I needed to sign the list because it was going to be submitted to the owners very soon. Now, when I got the list, I immediately noticed that out of 50 people, everyone chose The Outback Restaurant as the place they wanted the celebration to be held. The Outback would be a smart choice because it was convenient since it was within walking distance from the firm. And, coincidently, I consider The Outback as one of my very favorite restaurants. Apparently, everyone shared that same opinion because some people didn't even write the name; instead, they just put the little quotation "ditto" marks to signify "same as above."

When I wrote down my choice of restaurants, I put "Cheesecake Factory." I didn't think much of anything about my choice. It was a reflex action. I was simply honestly responding to the question, "Where would you prefer to go?" Anyway, when the list was handed to one of the managers to give to the owners, someone who observed the list (I remember it was a female) said quite loudly, "Who put Cheesecake Factory? Oh ...that's just CJ trying to be different!" I didn't say anything because The Outback would have been just fine with me. Besides, majority rules, doesn't it?

A few minutes later, I must admit, unexpectedly, one of the owners came and announced that it would be "a great idea" for us to celebrate at the Cheesecake Factory. "The Outback is practically right across the street. Some of us eat there twice a week for lunch. Why not go to the Cheesecake Factory? Good choice, CJ," he said. Before you know it, some of my coworkers were coming up to me, congratulating me as if I were some kind of hero. There were even others who were commenting that they should have made another choice themselves. All the while, I was somewhat surprised because this was no big deal to me; I was merely expressing what was on my mind.

B. Have the Courage To Bring Whatever You Have To The Table": Another True Story Example

Once, while working at a different company during the Thanksgiving Holiday season, before the break, my individual unit—which consisted of about 15 people—decided to have our own celebration luncheon because the company as a whole, being politically correct (or "incorrect," depending on how one looks at it), wouldn't sponsor a company-wide luncheon. Not everyone in the unit participated; nor did every unit in the company hold such event (Some people took personal time off for the holidays to go out of town, etc). Nevertheless, as common with these type of events, everyone would be responsible for bringing some kind of food item or whatever was necessary. There was fried turkey, homemade dressing, (some people use "stuffing" instead), mac-n-cheese, vegetables, desserts, etc. (I brought fried chicken myself.) Anyway, you name it, we had too much food for so few people. But there was one main item missing: Believe it or not, as we were preparing for our feast, someone noticed that there was no cranberry sauce! I remember saying out loud, "You have got to be kidding me!

Now, we had scheduled this event to be held at all participants' official lunch time, so no one really had to use some of their time leaving to go get cranberry sauce. While we were discussing who, if anyone, was going to get cranberry sauce (to some it didn't matter), there was a lady in the break room from another unit who heard about our dilemma. A few minutes later, she came back with 2 cans of cranberry sauce. "What a beautiful lady!" I thought. Consequently, the lady was happily invited to sit at the table and join in on our feast. While every participant in our unit had spent money buying items and/or spent maybe $3 and it was—at least to myself and some others—the most significant contribution at the table.

IV. BE OPEN MINDED TO OTHER POINTS OF VIEWS
(and have the integrity to admit when you're wrong)

In my opinion, in general, the largest problem with most religions and their followers is that they too often think they have all the answers. Let me let you in on a little secret: No one has all the answers! "It" (this phenomenon we call "the supernatural") is not designed for any one person or religion to have all the answers. Even Jesus Christ asked questions of his Heavenly Father! Nevertheless, some religions and their religious followers are worse than others when it comes to their self-perceived superiority.

There was a show on TV in the break room on the CNN channel reporting on a topic related to Islam. "Brooklyn commented to me something to the effect that he considered Islam as an evil religion and that a Muslim shouldn't try to have anything to say to him. This comment drew agreeable and disagreeable reactions from other people in the break room who overheard it. I guess I was so compelled that, without thinking, I asked, "So if Jesus Christ was walking around knowingly in our presence today, and he was approached by a known Muslim, do you think he'd sit down and hold a conversation with him?" Not waiting for an answer and not even really wanting an answer, and definitely not wanting confrontation, I immediately left the break room, I've never known what was said by whom in that break room after I left. All I know is that, later, "Brooklyn" came over to my desk (Our desks were on opposite sides of the office) and said, "Alright, C J, you got that one. You were right. But, you didn't have to embarrass me." I paused and said quietly, but emphatically, "My man, perhaps you embarrassed yourself!"

We need to realize that with any subject, especially when it comes to matters concerning the master plan of The Most High God, whose actions we are not fully capable of understanding; no religion has all the answers. Therefore, we should keep our minds open to other points of views because, perhaps all religions have some truths. Let's remember, someone somewhere once said (paraphrasing): "A fool is a person who thinks he has all the answers while a wise man knows he can always learn something new."

V. DON'T BE AFRAID TO TAKE RISKS

As we contemplate our quest towards enlightenment (however we define the term), we have to realize and understand that those who gain enlightenment don't usually achieve it easily. Usually, they are willing to take risks. There is a saying: "Many are called, but few are chosen." Many times, the ones that end up being chosen are the ones willing to endure the journeys complete with obstacles, trials, and tribulations that most people prefer to avoid. Many people will join the "cause" or "jump on the bandwagon," but few will take the initiative to direct a cause or make a change. Listen, I'm not advocating that we approach life and decision-making hap-hazardly (or "get slap happy" as my Dad might say) or that we "take wooden nickels" as my Mother might say) without working out the logistics and calculating all alternatives and thinking about the consequences. However, I am suggesting that sometimes there comes a window in time that an opportunity comes along or a situation presents itself just right for you to take advantage of the experience if you're willing to take the risks.

C. J. Johnson received his BA degree from the University of North Florida.

Rev. Goodlow and the Saturday Night Student Preachers

By
Richard D. Ashe

For decades Stillman College was known for producing quality and prominent ministers. For the most part, my recollection of the ministerial students who I had the privilege to meet and observe had impeccable character traits. To a large extent the ministerial students were considered as "goodwill ambassadors of the college." Although the author's intent of this story is to highlight the positive aspects of the ministerial students who I personally knew, it behooves and saddens me to also mention the behavior of an individual who betrayed the ministerial student image.

This "so called ministerial student' was given the title of "Rev. Goodlow" by his peers because they observed that he was very good at being a "lowdown, two-faced, scheming liar." Rev. Goodlow attended Stillman with the financial backing, prayers and well wishes of his hometown community and other scholarship agencies. However, Rev. Goodlow never intended for the ministry to become his vocation.

Although he masqueraded himself as a ministerial student, his behavior and respect for the program never came close to the standards of other ministerial students, such as Alex Chambers, Linton Gunn, Isaac Crosby, Frederick Blackburn, Joe Rigsby, William Jones, Vernon Swift, Lawrence Haygood, and Larry E.Williams.

Rev. Goodlow could deliver a warm and heart stirring sermon at churches where he was invited to preach. His favorite time was when a love offering was taken up for him. His peers knew that his sermons never came from a true, kindhearted and sincere person. They also knew that while he exploited the system for financial gain, they also observed how he would seize opportunities to take advantage of numerous young ladies by making false promises of hope. Rev. Goodlow was quick to make commitments to young ladies in the Tuscaloosa area, but in reality, he was already in a committed relationship back home.

It was common knowledge that student ministers would often receive invitations to deliver the morning worship service message at local churches in the area. During my freshman year I discovered that a regular church style service was conducted every Saturday evening on the bottom floor in the men's dormitory of John Knox Hall.

I felt honored when one of the student ministers invited me to be a guest at one of their church services held in one of the student minister's dormitory room. At the designated time, I entered the room and was directed to sit with two other invited guests. The program began with one of the ministerial students informing the visitors of the evening's program and procedures. We were informed that there student ministers had been assigned for the month to deliver a weekly well constructed sermon within a ten minute time span. We were also told that their denominational title was a weekly rotational assignment. For instance the Presbyterian, Methodist, and Baptist ministers for that evening's sermon would be assigned to deliver a sermon under a different denomination at the following Saturday Night Service.

We were informed that the following student ministers would be delivering sermons during the evening: Arthur McFadden, Alvin Taylor and Lenton Gunn, Jr. The topic of each student minister's sermon would be, "Issues Facing Students during Controversial Times." We were also told that if the spirit moves the invited guest to speak during the service by saying "Amen," it would be appropriate to do so.

The first student minister to speak was introduced as the Pastor of **"John Knox Hall Presbyterian Church."** (John Knox Hall was the men's dormitory on campus) The speaker gave a highly motivational presentation within the specified ten minute time frame. The delivery of the sermon was presented masterfully. At the conclusion of his presentation the invited guest made remarks such as "Very good," "Right on," "Great job."

The second student minister to speak on the topic was introduced as the Pastor of **Birthright Auditorium Methodist Church.** (Birthright Auditorium was the multipurpose gymnasium on campus). The speaker adequately defined the topic and gave the audience (guests) possible solutions for coping with the issues that were being presented.

During this sermon there were a couple of "Yes," and one "Amen." At the conclusion of the sermon, the speaker received a hearty applause for his efforts.

The third and final student minister to speak was introduced as the pastor of **Sheppard Library Baptist Church.** (Sheppard Library was the name of the campus library) I thought it was interesting and creative of the student ministers to add a church denomination to campus buildings and call them churches. This added a little extra spice to the occasion. The Baptist speaker had a high pitched baritone voice. He also gave examples of how the issues presented in the evening's topic would somehow affect everyone in the room. Throughout this student minister's sermon, words such as, "Amen," "Preach the word," and, "yeah" were used. Reaction from the invited guests also produced foot stomping and standing shouts of approval.

At the conclusion of the sermons the guest gave a thunderous applause to the student ministers for their efforts. The other invited guests and I realized that these same student ministers at next week's Saturday Night Service would be presented as pastors of another denomination and their speech delivery would probably be different from that evening's delivery. The sermon topic would also be different.

The invited guests thanked the student ministers for their invitation and encouraged them to continue to provide well prepared and inspiring sermons. I requested that they consider me for another invitation as soon as their rules would allow it. I left the room thinking that the three ministerial students that spoke that evening were destined to become prominent ministers and Stillman College alumni.

MAGNOLIA POETRY

"Be forever mindful that no person or situation can keep you from achieving your goals and aspirations unless you allow it to happen."

R. D. Ashe

CHAPTER SEVEN

Magnolia Poetry
Magnolia Trees

Since the founding of Stillman College in 1876, many beautiful and long-standing landmarks have been noted on the campus. One of the most outstanding and gracious of those landmarks is Stillman's Magnolia Trees. As long as anyone can remember, the Magnolia Trees have stood to tell the story of Stillman College.

The age of the Magnolia Trees has not been determined. The closest approximate age has been estimated to be over 100 years. Passers-by have observed the picturesque scene of the four magnificent highly enchanting magnolias symmetrically arranged on the lawn of the library building. These magnolias, to some, are mere representatives of pretty trees or to an artist they are the essence of a beautiful scene exhilarating in their tranquility, encompassed in mysticism and heart rendering in their sentimentality.

Richard D. Ashe, Ph.D

But perhaps the best way to describe the magnolias is captured in a poem written by Laurence Haygood, a 1955 graduate of Stillman College. His poem is entitled "The Old Magnolia Tree."

"The Old Magnolia Tree"

When I first came to Stillman,
Many building were new to me;
The first thing I observed
Was the Old Magnolia Tree.
Behind the Office Building
She proudly stands--
Without a single worry-
Calm in this confused land
Always quiet and peaceful,
She beckons us to relax and to pray.
She looks at the Fellowship House
And calls "fellowman" all the day.
Undisturbed by storm, and unbent by age
Nor afraid of the shadows of darkness
When night falls;
'She is serene, and brave, and free.
Oh how I wish I could be
Like the Old Magnolia Tree.

- Laurence Haygood

From College Archieves-1974-Robert Heath, College archivist

A FATHER'S GIFT TO HIS CHILDREN

(A motivational and poetic essay)

I

My children, I have been blessed with the opportunity
to watch and protect you from infancy to puberty.
You are now on the threshold to be an independent young man
and woman.
As you spread your wings, and face the morning and evening sun
You will find some encounters will not always be fair or fun.

Hurdles and tribulations will confront you face to face.
That's the price everyone pays to be part of this imperfect place.
My dear children, I offer you a solid guidepost with a few tips
To help you during your uncertain journey and trip.

II

Keep these inspirational words of wisdom close to your breast
Because they are as valuable as jewels from a treasure chest.

Through your upcoming journey into the passageway of adulthood,
Take the armor and teachings of the Prince of Power and Peace,
They will allow unbearable attacks to cease and give you peace.

You have learned a great deal within the short span of your life.
You still have a lot to learn. Wisdom will come as you age,
Knowledge will be acquired through your experiences.
At times you may have to work from trouble trenches.

III

The troubled times you face can become a blessing in disguise.
View the circumstances in a positive slant for the good that could
Bring about personal triumph and pride.

Regardless of how much you want to achieve, or noble your cause,
Circumstances will test your strength and the spirit of your soul.

To an extent, the difference between failure and success lies in the
Changing of the words, "I won't" and "I can't" to "I can and I will."
This type of attitude will allow a lot of dreams to be fulfilled.

IV

Remember the words of Thomas Edison when asked whether he was
Discouraged because of so many attempts had failed. He would say,
"I am not discouraged because every wrong attempt discarded is
Another step forward."

Be mindful that no person or situation can keep you from achieving
Your goals and aspirations unless you allow it to happen.

If you should become content with the progress that you have made,
You rob yourself and others of additional pleasures and rewards.
If you fail to utilize your talents and skills,
Loose them you will.

V

When circumstances arise that cause conflict, find common ground
To reach a compromise. Not only is this the civilized way,
It's the right thing to do every day.

Treat everyone with dignity and respect because kindness and positive
Energy forces will broaden your horizon to useful and favorable ways
In your upcoming days.

You can become successful as much as you desire because you are
King and Queen of your destiny. All that is required is that you
Believe in you.

VI

"**B**elieve in yourself and your abilities. There are lots of other folks
Who will tell you, it can't be done."[1]

"**D**o what you can to show you care about other people, and you will make
Our world a better place."2

"**T**o excel is to reach your highest dream. But you must also help others to
Achieve theirs."3

"**R**emember, "Success is not defined by the number of servants you have,
But by how many people you serve."4

"**D**on't let the sun go down without putting sunshine in someone's life through Words or deeds. Remember, little things really count"5

"**K**eep away from people who try to belittle your ambitions. Small people always
Do that, but the really great make you feel that you too can become great."6

"**W**ith the Prince of Power and Peace by your side, be bold! Set positive and Constructive goals. Then implement your plans and plan to advance."7

1. Jasmine Guy, 2. Rosalyn Carter, 3. Barbara Walters, 4. Ralph D. Abernathy,
5. Richard D. Ashe, 6. Mark Twain, 7. Richard D. Ashe

Richard D. Ashe

THE EXTRAORDINARY MAN

I'm an Extraordinary Man. If you don't know it yet,
You may get lucky and take a trip on my private jet.
I am twice as talented as Denzel Washington;
More photogenic than General George Washington.

To win admirers over to my point of view,
I know precisely how to get things started to stew.
I can capture them with my good looks,
Or dazzle their instincts with my bank books.

Flaunting my attributes is unnecessary the least,
But I am a good looking hunk and loveable beast.
Egotism or being a brash braggart is not relevant here,
Factual or self assurance should not raise any fears.

When sophisticated ladies see me, they go wild,
But preying on ladies will never be my style.
After looking me over and checking me out,
They see and learn what I'm really about.

First and foremost, women are a blessing to mankind.
They are essential for possibilities to rise and shine.
Experience taught me that something is not much
Without a woman's touch.

Although I am known to be an Extraordinary Man,
I need everyone's help to implement a survival plan.
Our country will fall if we fail to take a stand.
I refer you to the plague that blights our land.

Attention is needed in areas of poverty, crime, education,
employment, incarnations, race relations
and media misinformation.
America remains a jewel among nations of the world,
Do we allow negligence to tarnish the world's pearl?

Do not judge me by the number of women notched,
But by the goodness and lives touched on my watch.
I am pleased and blessed to be an Extraordinary Man.
I hope you will become one of my fans
And support the causes for which I stand.

Richard Ashe

USE TO MEMORIES

I use to have lots of hair
Now my head is bald and bare.
I use to see distances near and far
My eyes now are like used up cars.

I use to run very fast
Now my legs feel like cement casts
Ladies use to smile at my physique and charm
Right now, they don't look, they only yawn.

I use to turn lots of lady's heads
Currently, I have difficulty turning my own head.
I use to generate instantaneous power
Now I'm lucky to have energy at any hour.

My feet were fast and ready to go
Now they go if I walk very slow.
I use to know your face and name
Now you all look the same.

I use to own my own beautiful teeth.
Now I own beautiful false teeth.
I use to dance all night
Now, being in bed early is my joy and delight.

If I could turn back the hand of time for some of
Those wild and mischievous days,
I'd put them in a bottle and save them for
Days like today.

Richard D. Ashe

Off With The Mask

The hidden and built up pain of 250 years of shame
Is rather difficult to explain.

But put away the mask of grins and lies
That covered our face and eyes.

It is a tribute to our intuition and mortal guile,
Although troubled with agonized hearts, we smiled.

The world was not at our side,
They saw not our tears, or heard our sighs.

Now let them see us without the pretense,
Off with the mask.

We glorify our Lord, He heard our cries
and allowed our anguished souls to arise.

We sing, but the enemy changes its colors and style.
The struggle continues, so away with guile,

Overcoming today's obstacles should be our main task
So,
Off with the mask.

Richard D. Ashe

* A response and update to Paul Laurence Dunbar's "We Wear The Mask."
** Reference: Soulful Poetry by this author, 1998.

BELIEVE

When someone or situations knock you to the ground
Pick yourself up with faith and determination,
You can turn the struggle around.

Even if your victimizer is determined to keep you down,
Use common sense with a positive action plan,
Then work your plan till it's solid and sound.

Success is failure turned inside out,
Victory will not come if you're tangled in clouds
Of doubt.

Goals or help will not come if you lack the desire,
You must be willing to fight with the right kind of fire.

Have confidence in the wisdom of universal laws and
The fundamental principle of the mind.
Increase your desire and know that you can achieve.

Amazingly, you must be willing to believe,
Your achievements will be measured by the size of your belief.
There is quality in every situation. If you believe and proceed
You will find relief and peace.

With your head up, shoulders straight, smile on your face,
Go forth.
With you is the Supreme Force to get you back on course.
When the battle is over, you will win and stand tall
As a role model for all.

Richard D. Ashe

* Reference: <u>Soulful Poetry</u> by this author, 1998

Richard D. Ashe, Ph.D

FAT AND FINE

I see you looking and laughing at my fat body.
The truth is you're jealous that I possess more than you.
You see, I may be fat, baby, but I'm fine.

Food is my middle name, and eating is my claim to fame.
I don't eat to live but live to eat.

My head, neck, thighs, and legs are all widespread.
In fact, one arm is larger than most people's two thighs.
Yes, baby, I may be fat, but I'm fine.

Give me some more of those pork chops,
Bar-B-Que ribs, black eyed peas, and beans.
I'll have a side order of heavy buttered cornbread
And spicy collard greens.

For dessert, I'll have cheese cake, strawberries,
And peach cobbler, with a pint size topping of
Pure vanilla ice cream.

High blood pressure, breathing heavy and not being
Able to see the top of my shoes is a way of life
Due to food abuse.
So what! I may be fat, but I'm fine!

Richard D. Ashe

* Reference: <u>Poetic Expressions </u>by this author, 1995

CHICKEN FAN MAN

Fish, steak, and ribs are okay for some, but not for me
Eating chicken meals is where I always want to be.
I won't deny, I love chicken very much and that's no lie
Frequently, I have my lips and teeth in a leg, breast or thigh.

When I get out of bed, I'm looking for a chicken leg
Until I finish this task, my ears will not hear whatever is said.
Mama and Papa love chicken too. They specialize in chicken stew
When cooked, we all begin to eat like a bunch of greedy fools.

Chicken soup, chicken salad, chicken fried rice, or chicken pie
Chicken lovers don't complain if chicken is baked, broiled or fried.
Anyone not liking chicken must be from Mars or live in a hole
For me, I'll do anything for a helping of chicken. It's like gold.

I'll bear any burden and pay the cost wherever chicken is sold
All over the world the goodness and taste of chicken should be told.
I'm changing my first and last name. Changed to be –"Chicken Man"
The reasoning is simple. I am and will always be a chicken fan man.

Richard D. Ashe

Richard D. Ashe, Ph.D

SWEET POTATO PIE

I eat sweet potato pie in the morning, noon and night,
If I don't get it, my body isn't quite right.
I want sweet potato pie when I work, drive or fly.
All I ever want and need is sweet potato pie.

When I'm given a piece of sweet potato pie,
You should know that one piece doesn't fit my stomach size.
I always ask for more, more and more,
Simply because sweet potato pie is what I adore.

It matters not if I'm at the great cathedral in Rome,
Or if I'm attending a sports event inside of a dome;
Eating sweet potato pie is like a king sitting on a throne.
It's also better than watching TV or talking on the telephone.

If I should ever look like I'm getting sick,
For emergency reasons, get me some sweet potato pie real quick.
Don't call a doctor, nurse or get me medicated pills,
For me, sweet potato pie will cure whatever makes me ill.

When I leave this earth, open a bottle of blueberry wine;
Serving sweet potato pie will also be fine and divine.
Remember me for loving God and everything under the sky;
And of course, for having a big appetite for sweet potato pie.

Richard D. Ashe

EUPHIZINE

Euphizine grew up in the sleepy, Carolina Mountains,
It was common to have picnics and family outings
Then she moved to the busy and bustling city of Baltimore
Her charm and wisdom had not been apparent before.

Elegance with glamorous appeal had never been seen
until the emergence of the adorable Euphizine.
In grade school her fashion stood out among the rest
Everyone knew that she would have the prettiest dress.

Most times one could predict her head would dawn a pair,
A pair of colorful ribbons fastened to her hair.
Working with noble causes and putting pep in her steps
She'd catch the attention of strangers who wanted to help.

Summer plans include time at her childhood home
Where family, friends and neighbors love to roam,
Evenings and family time include sitting on the porch,
It has become fun to watch fluffy clouds for sport.

Friends, family, and extended family, all agree
Euphizine has always been spiritual and busy as a bee,
Praising the Almighty, and doing for others to succeed
Is what Euphizine always wants to achieve.

Just as a courtroom bailiff urges everyone to stand
Earthly and heavenly angels honor her and also stand.
Beauty and wisdom with exceptional skills are rarely seen
But they all mesh together in our matriarch, Euphizine.

Richard D. Ashe

FALL TREES AND BEAUTIFUL LEAVES

Trees and leaves in the fall begin to display their glittering wares,
They display their leafy best with other trees before going bare.
Like a festival on display they become part of trees on parade,
In the fall they provide more than refuge in the shade.

Nature lines them up to display their finest and colorful best,
Judges would pass them with flying colors if they were taking a test.
Colorful trees of all species work in harmony for the yearly display,
Mother Nature may be showing beings of all nations how to behave.

The trees and leaves appear to punctuate their individual style,
Collectively they show their glitzy colors with charm and a smile.
They seem to say "Look at me with my fine and fancy leaves,
Stop, stare, study, get to know and enjoy me."

When leaves reach their brightest peak, they flitter to the ground,
Shortly they turn the same color and transform to a chocolate brown.
Leaves help to enrich the soil for nature to display its fleeting toy,
Fall trees and beautiful leaves work in unison for all of us to enjoy.

Richard D. Ashe

GUNS

There's a Bang Bang here
a Bang Bang there.
Everywhere there's a Bang Bang.

There's a dead body here
a dead body there.
Everywhere there's a dead body.

FUN, FUN, FUN!
NO!
DUMB, DUMB, DUMB! *

Richard D. Ashe

* Reference: <u>Poetic Expressions</u> by this author, 1995

"Mama's Ten Commandments"

1. Don't let me have to come up to that school.

2. Be sure that you are wearing clean underwear.

3. Don't shame me by being shameful.

4. Don't bring something in here you can't take care of .

5. Wash under your arms and around your bottom.

6. Be careful with who you hang around with.

7. Keep your dress down and your underwear pulled up.

8. Go and act like you got some sense.

9. Keep your thing inside of your pants.

10. What go on inside of this house stays in this house.

Richard D. Ashe

* Source: (Play, 2011) **"Judgment Day at Pearlie Gate Court"**

NEW ORLEANS, AFTER KATRINA
(For the survivors of Hurricane Katrina)

I

Katrina, before you came, I could pick up a pen and write with ease,
I was blessed with the ability to craft "Poetic Expressions."
Any subject matter I chose to write about was a breeze,
You caused millions to have self reflections, and wish for connections.

II

Like so many victims of your destruction, I was also traumatized,
My mind would not allow me to write a word about you.
Individuals who failed to heed your approach risked their demise,
Your destruction and deaths that you caused were more than just a few.

III

After you calmed down, the levees broke sending water to roof tops,
Dead bodies, dead animals, and toxic waste floated all around.
Officials had failed to take safety measures and connect appropriate dots,
The people struggled to get to higher ground.

IV

Thousands of desperate and dying were at the Super Dome,
Five days they called for the president, governor, and mayor for assistance.
Katrina, chaos and fear ruled shortly after you had gone,
While crossing a bridge to safety, police officers responded with resistance.

V

New Orleans, a great city was under water; the blame game had begun,
Finger pointing was in high gear, officials refused to take the blame,
They didn't want to be condemned for the worst disaster under the sun,
Katrina, the devastation and incredible human suffering was yours
to claim.

VI

Katrina, your visit caused us lots of grief and pain,
The New Orleans as we knew it will never be the same.
For better or worse the city continues to change,
The nation's pride and love for this great city will always remain.

VII

Katrina, will the power structure strive for racial and economic justice?
Did you cause us to look at ourselves as a caring nation?
What policy changes could cause the world to take notice?
Katrina, will good ultimately emerge from this tragic situation?

Richard D. Ashe

RABBITS ARE EVERY WHERE

There's a rabbit over here
There's a rabbit over there
Rabbits are seen every where,
You'd better beware,
Goodness gracious!
There's a hare in your hair!

TURNING HEADS

Old Timer: When I was a young man,
I turned the heads of many ladies.

Young Timer: Sir, you can still turn lots of heads.

Old Timer: How can that possibly be?

Young Timer: Just open your wallet
and let your money spread.
Nothing else needs to be said.

Richard D. Ashe

I'm Alive, I'm Not Dead Yet
(For Senior Citizen Men)

The forecast of my imminent demise has been revised,
I am well and getting better.
I've made interesting plans. Relatives likely will chatter.
So what, I'm not dead yet and that's all that matters.

Thanks to the Almighty and all those blue pills,
My bones are telling me to get ready for thrills.
My head is white as snow; my hormones want to flow,
The fire in my body furnace says lets go!

Richard D. Ashe

Richard D. Ashe, Ph.D

A RADICAL SLAVE SPEAKS FROM THE GRAVE

I

For over 300 years I've observed events from my dusty casket
At times situations have tempted me to grab a club or hatchet
I follow events in Georgia, Mississippi and Alabama
I served slave masters in each of these states.

II

There was no mercy for slaves who tried to escape
Being treated as though we weren't human was our fate
I sent a petition to angels in heaven to send slave owners to hell
I feel that slave owners or supporters aren't fit for jail.

III

In Mississippi to this day, they refuse to honor Abraham Lincoln
He freed slaves from shackles and chains
But they honor Robert E. Lee who wanted slave laws to remain
This mind set is disrespectful and a shame.

IV

I tried to persuade the gate keepers of heaven to let me in
But my arguments and pleas did not let me win
They said I was too radical and had an unforgiving heart
My fellow cemetery mates say my views aren't very smart.

V

Well, I'm not forgiving and I'm not forgetting
Even if I have to remain in this cemetery setting
My idea is to see some restitution and pay back
For all those horrifying slave attacks.

VI

I want slave owners and their supporters brought back to life
I want their suffering to be the slaves delight
May they be led daily to cow pastures and made to kiss
the lips and feet of pigs, skunks, goats and cows. This is my wish.

VII

My petition and desire for revenge may someday come true
If not, I got nothing to loose
I'll be content to lie here in my grave and sing the blues.

Richard D. Ashe

ARTHRITIS ON THE RUN

For centuries arthritis has had his way with senior citizens
This monster grabs strong bones and makes them weak
There is no mercy or courtesy for the humble or meek
Once he touches your body, your soul aches for weeks.

His pain manifests inside your body year after year
Then he goes after your loved ones and others who are dear
This devil laughs when he sees his prey in unbearable pain
His goal is to make everyone cripple and lame.

I believe its time to put arthritis on the run
His attacks have been compared to needles and guns
When he assaults us, all we can do is moan
I say to one and all, its time for him to be gone.

If this thug tries to enter my body or touch my rump
I'll give him a gut wrenching thump
I won't let up until he's placed inside a pen
Arthritis won't be released until he repents from his sins.

Richard D. Ashe

ILLUSIONS OF AN OLD MAN

Here I stand on my front porch near the street,
What's aching now are my two swollen feet.
Further down the road, I hear musical sounds
of a lively beat. They remind me of youthful
feats.

Every now and then I see a young lady walking or
driving by.
When this happens, my heart throbs as though
It wants to jump to the sky.

I dream of the day when technology could put
energy back into my heart, head and legs.
Then faster, I'll be able to move, sooth and get
back into my groove.

If medical scientist would hurry up, maybe one day
I'll be able to talk faster, run, dance and sway.
With young ladies, I'd be able to play.

Just the thought that this could happen excites me.
It's like fire inside of me that wants to be free
I feel as though I'm having another heart attack,
So I'd better sit down and try to relax.

Richard D. Ashe

MISS UPPITY THANG

There she is again; I'm talking about Miss Uppity Thang.
For some, she's a thorn and pain
For others, they love to watch that fine brown frame.
Her head and nose are turned up in the air
Many wish for her time to spare and share.

When she walks, her hips always sway and glide
From side to side
If you don't have tons of money and a title by your name
It's useless trying to impress her with your play or game
She's an intellectual super star,
She can out think the average Joe way by far.

If you cross her, just look for a drop kick to the other side
She can give creative swift kicks to one's behind
It matters not if yours is narrow or wide.
My brother, do you wish to abide,
Or let your chances go right on by?

Richard D. Ashe

THE TRAGIC DEATH OF KATHRYN JOHNSON

I

My friends and fellow citizens, weep with me,
Death came and took away a saintly elder,
Circumstances regarding her demise are hard to believe,
Due to Kathryn Johnson's passing, we mourn together.

II

Listen and read how her story is told,
Take note of how this beautiful life unfolds,
Participants in this episode were bold;
Evil deeds done in darkness eventually showed.

III

The eighty eight year old elder loved flowers,
She welcomed the rain that came in showers,
Solving word puzzles, she enjoyed for hours,
Reading the Bible increased her strength and power.

IV

Kathryn Johnson resided at 933 Neal Street,
Around the corner and in her neighborhood
Walkers or riders could see her flowery treat;
Dope dealers and seekers searched for goods.

V

Residents barred windows and shut their doors tight,
They knew the routine of dope addicts,
Usually dope freaks came out at night,
At times their behavior would become erratic.

VI

The snitch said drugs were at her address,
Officers prepared their ill- fated attack;
Delighted officers wanted to make a major arrest

While armed to the teeth with bogus facts.

VII

The drug squad sought to have unusual luck
Rather than factual details while seeking proof;
It mattered not if warrants were made up,
Their mission was not about justice or truth.

VIII

To find drugs, they entered with guns a blazing,
The elderly body was sprawled over her bed,
The force used was incomprehensible and amazing,
Blood splattered on walls and above her head.

IX

They engineered lies that very hellacious night,
Officers decided, "We must now plant some weed."
They prepared to hide truth from the light.
"We'll report she was dealing with poisonous weed."

X

This time, ordinary routine underscores their tasks,
Their brazen scheme would be their last,
This death uncovered a police force's ugly mask,
False charges of innocent individuals unraveled fast.

XI

Questions about the police began to fly,
This drug bust refused to die,
Skeptics believed the police report was a lie;
Anger, demands, and demonstrations were wide.

XII

An eighty- eight year old woman selling drugs!
Unlikely the least and sinister at best,
Would factual evidence be swept under the rug?
And would truth overcome the "blue code test?

XIV

While we earthly mortals were shocked and mourned
Some compared this death to Sherman's March,
Heavenly angels prepared her saintly wings to adorn;
Atlanta added another indelible impression to its watch:
Host to the Summer Olympic Games
"Deadly bomb blast in Olympic Park
"The city too busy to hate"
"The black Mecca of the south"
"The Atlanta Teenage Murders"
"A want to be international city"
The Narcotics Department received little sympathy or pity.

XV

Oh how truth crushed to the earth rises!
The commissioner found the officers' reports didn't match,
The community called for action without compromises,
The FBI was summoned to sort out facts.

XVI

A frightened snitch called a television station,
"Crooked cops want me to take the fall."
The snitch's words were heard around the nation,
"Protect me; I've done nothing wrong at all."

XVII

Kathryn Johnson's executioners were sentenced to jail,
For several years, they will be in a cell,
Some wished for the officers to rot in hell,
Others felt that justice turned out well.

XVIII

Kathryn Johnson has gone on to glory,
What lessons can be taught or learned?
How and who will tell her story?
Is there a need to be concerned?

XIX

Is it far fetched for one's imagination
For citizens to say:
Establish a Kathryn Johnson Police Foundation?
What do you think? What do you say?

Richard D. Ashe

PEOPLE, PLACES AND THINGS DURING 1963

**"What legacy will you leave behind?
Will it be one that allows others to climb?"**

R.D. Ashe

CHAPTER EIGHT

People, Places and Things
Fifty Years Ago

Nineteen Sixty Three was an historic year for the graduates of Stillman College. They received a Bachelors Degree during Commencement. These graduates also observed historic events that concerned the entire country during this period of time. Therefore, Chapter Seven seeks to give the reader a brief synopsis of specific occurrences of that year. Chapter Seven also gives recognition to the Golden Year (50th) Anniversary of the 1963 graduates.

George Wallace Takes a Stand

On June 11, 1963 Governor George Wallace symbolically stood in the doorway at the University of Alabama to defy a federal desegregation order to allow the enrollment of two black students. That night President John F. Kennedy gave an extraordinary speech to the nation regarding the incident. In his speech, he stated, "Their peaceful admission on campus is due in good measure to the conduct of the students of the University of Alabama"...

"This Nation was founded by men of many nations and backgrounds. It was founded on the principle that all men are created equal, and that the rights of every man are diminished when the rights of one man are threatened."

The 16th Street Baptist Church Bombing

The Sixteenth Street Baptist Church in Birmingham, Alabama was used as a meeting place for civil rights leaders such as Martin Luther King Jr., Ralph David Abernathy and Fred Shuttlesworth.

On Sunday, September 15, 1963, a man placed a bomb under the steps of the church. At 10:22 a.m. the bomb exploded killing four children; Addie Mae Collins, Carole Robertson, Cynthia Wesley, and Denise McNair.

1963 HISTORICAL FACTS

World Series Baseball champions-----------Los Angeles Dodgers
National Football champions-----Chicago Bears
National Basketball champions---------Boston Celtics
NCAA Football champions---------University of Texas
The most popular movie stars: Elizabeth Taylor, Jayne Mansfield, Audrey Hepburn and Kim Novak.
"The Quote" from Dallas, Texas, "President Kennedy died at 1 p.m."
Time Magazine's Man of the Year----Martin Luther King Jr.

June 17 The Supreme Court ruled that laws requiring the citing of the Lord's Prayer or Bible verse in public schools were unconstitutional.

The first boxer to earn one million dollars was Sonny Liston. He defeated Floyd Patterson.
Dr. James Hardy performed the first lung transplant.

MOST POPULAR T V SHOWS

1. Beverly Hillbillies
2. Bonanza
3. The Dick Van Dyke Show
4. Petticoat Junction
5. Andy Griffin Show
6. The Lucy Show
7. The Danny Thomas Show
8. Candid Camera
9. The Ed Sullivan Show

Motown Superstar: Stevie Wonder (Finger Tips)
Popular Black Actresses: Dorothy Dandridge, Jayne Kennedy and Lena Horne

An Average Cost

A new home-----$19,300
First Class stamp-----.05
A gallon of regular gasoline -----0.30
A dozen of eggs-----0.55
A gallon of Milk-----0.49

*Source: Internet

FIFTY YEAR PICTORIAL REVIEW

"With your head up, shoulders straight and a smile on your face, go forth and be productive."

R. D. Ashe

IDENTIFY THE STILLMANITES ON THE PREVIOUS PAGES. DO YOUR BEST, THEN CALL A CLASSMATE OR FRIEND TO NAME THE REST.

A FINAL WORD

**WHEN SOMEONE OR SITUATIONS KNOCK YOU TO THE
GROUND
PICK YOURSELF UP WITH FAITH AND DETERMINATION,
YOU CAN TURN THE STRUGGLE
AROUND.**

R. D. Ashe

A FINAL WORD

Generally speaking, members of a board of trustees possess knowledge of current bylaws and policies of the institution they represent. They also have a fundamental grasp of rules, procedures and expectations of decisions made on behalf of the institution. Therefore, this author salutes the following past or present Stillman College Alumni members who have served on the Stillman College Board of Trustees; and have make decisions that are in the best interest of Stillman: Robert Burns, Eligah Clark, Gloria Dennard, Alfonso Denson, Dennis Driver, Evelyn Gunn, Eddie Johnson, Floyd Phillips, Lena Prewitt, Joseph Roulhac, Ann Simmons, Haywood Strickland, Betty Williamson, Alex Chambers, I. Logan Kearse, Sue Thompson, Michael Figures, Wardell Croft, Samuel Ethridge, Chaney Washington and Frank H. M. Williams.

Once again the author wishes to express his deepest appreciation to all the contributors who made it possible for **Under the Magnolia Tree** to become a literary reality. The efforts of the many individuals who gave their time, talents, suggestions and resources will help provide support for needy students at a designated HBCU school.

Website Information

Upon the completion of the magnolia book project, the author began to develop a "discussion /writing work book." The workbook will be for teachers, book club members and others who wish to enhance the discussion of articles and memories that have been shared in <u>Under The Magnolia Tree.</u>

To obtain information regarding the workbook and other writings by the author, visit the website: richarddashelegacymotivations.org

Phone: 404-502-4416

Email: rashe@bellsouth.net

Fax: 404-257-6402

Mailing Address:

1640 County Line Road, SW
Atlanta, GA 30331

GOING FORWARD

As the final words of **<u>Under The Magnolia Tree</u>** are being written, once again I wish to say thanks to all who gave of their time, talent and resources for this project. It is now time for me to embark upon another challenge. This writer envisions that the resources obtained from this book will be used to establish and/or assist scholarship programs for selected HBCU schools. Therefore, I am asking you, the reader to be a blessing to others by purchasing multiple copies of this book and distribute them to your friends, family and co-workers. Your actions will assist some college students to make their dreams become a reality.

Richard D. Ashe

Under The Magnolia Tree Donors

Benny Amin

Christina Ashe

Leonard Ashe

Marvin C. & Cynthia Ashe

Verna Bourgeois

Rose Buggs

Lula Cox

Christine Davis

Ruth Dunn

Ethel M. Fairley

Sandra Fletcher

Charles Gamble

Sharmain Green

Jane C. Griffin

Charlie G. & Lola Hardy

Alice B. Hamilton

Delores Hampton

Cleveland Holmes

Frederick W. & Yvette Hudson

Shirley Jackson

Martha Jefferson

James Johnson

Juanita Lamar

Clarence Lewis

Eddie B. May

Benard & Dorthy McCants

Vilmer M. Meyer

Gloria Morgan

Colin & Dee Hall Nelson

Emma Newkirk

Susie Norris

Edward North Sr.

Asa E. Owens

Yeolman Owens

Richard D. Ashe, Ph.D

Phillip & Barbara Phinisee   Napoleon Suluke

Valerie M. Roberts   Beauregard Thomas

Clara Robinson   Louise Thomas

Juanita Ross   Thelma Towns

Gerold Selby   Dolores Walker

Shirley Stanley   Charlotte A. Wilkins

Claude Stines   Ella F. Young

INDEX